D1083895

A Political Geography of Community Europe

A Political Geography of Community Europe

Geoffrey Parker, MA, DipEd, FRGS
Lecturer, Department of Extramural Studies, University of Birmingham

Butterworths
London Boston Durban Singapore Sydney Toronto Wellington

First published 1983

© Geoffrey Parker, 1983

British Library Cataloguing in Publication Data

Parker, Geoffrey
  A political geography of Community Europe.
  1. European Economic Community
  I. Title
  341.24′22   HC241.2

  ISBN 0-408-10839-8

Library of Congress Cataloging in Publication Data

Parker, Geoffrey, 1933–
  A political geography of Community Europe.
  Includes index.
  1. European Communities.
  2. Geopolitics – Europe.
  I. Title
  JN15.P34 1983   341.24′2   83-6054

  ISBN 0-408-10839-8

Photoset by Butterworths Litho Preparation Department
Printed and bound in Great Britain by Mackays of Chatham Ltd, Chatham, Kent.

Preface

The object of this book is to examine the political geography of 'Community Europe' with a view to ascertaining the extent to which it has acquired, or is in course of acquiring, distinct geopolitical characteristics of its own. There has been a widespread tendency to think of 'The Community', also known popularly as 'The Common Market', in unitary terms. This tendency has been encouraged by developments which have taken place since the late 1960s. However, it is important always to be aware that legally there are three separate entities, those being the European Coal and Steel Community (ECSC), the European Economic Community (EEC) and the European Atomic Energy Community (EAEC), this latter known more familiarly as 'Euratom'. The correct collective title is therefore the plural 'European Communities' (EC), and it is this which is consequently used in this book when specific reference is being made to the institutions and to the organization as a whole. One of the features all three have in common is the same territorial extent, and the singular 'Community' is used when reference is intended to the geographical area and its features. The numbers in brackets after EC refer to the Communities at different periods. Thus EC(6) refers to the 'Community of Six' as it was between 1958 and 1972 and EC(10) to the situation following the second enlargement of 1981.

I wish to express my gratitude to the Information Services of the European Communities in both Brussels and Luxembourg for their ready assistance to me during the writing of this book. I also take pleasure in thanking my wife for her invaluable assistance throughout and for preparing the index. My thanks also go to Mrs J. Dowling, who so meticulously drew the accompanying maps and diagrams to the required specifications.

Geoffrey Parker
Lichfield

v

Contents

List of figures

List of tables

Chapter 1

A bold act: the search for peace by pieces

On 7 May 1945 World War II came to an end in Europe with the formal surrender of the German forces to the Allied Powers at Rheims. The Third Reich, for which its founders had predicted a long and glorious history, had ended in total defeat after only 13 years and the victorious 'Big Three' – the Grand Alliance of the United States, the United Kingdom and the Soviet Union – were in complete possession of its disorganized and devastated territories. This date also marked the effective end of the old Europe which had dominated the world for so long.

Almost exactly five years later, on 9 May 1950, the French Foreign Minister, Robert Schuman, speaking in the Salon de l'Horloge at the Quai d'Orsay in Paris, proposed that a start should be made on reconciling the old adversaries by bringing the coal and steel industries of France and Germany under a common authority. He called his proposal 'a leap into the unknown', and it was the beginning of the creation of a new Europe.

During the first half of 1945, first at Yalta and then at Potsdam, the Big Three had been faced with the daunting task of reconstructing Europe after six years of trauma and devastation. The Potsdam Conference[1] of July and August of that year unearthed more problems than it solved. Particularly acute were those arising from the *de facto* boundary changes brought about by the Russians in the lands which they had occupied. These centred on the annexation by Poland and, to a lesser degree, the Soviet Union of all German territories lying to the east of the Oder–Neisse rivers together with the redrawing of Poland's eastern boundary to follow roughly the old Curzon line[2]. Poland was thus compensated in the west at the expense of Germany for what she lost to the Soviets in the east. These and other changes had to be grudgingly accepted as *faits accomplis* by the Western powers, but the animosities engendered in Germany by the 'lost lands' issue were to bedevil European affairs for decades. There were also disagreements over the exact interpretation of 'democracy' as applied to the parts of Europe under Soviet control and the question of how to approach a solution to the problem of Germany. From then on the Western powers and the Soviet Union began to drift apart as more matters went unresolved, and it became clear that there were considerable

1

differences of opinion about the nature of the new Europe they were trying to create. Between the two great zones of influence and stretching from the North Cape of Norway to the shores of the Mediterranean an 'Iron Curtain'[3] had come down. Over the next five years contacts through it were to become gradually fewer, and its most sensitive section was that which cut right through the old centre of Germany dividing the Soviet zone from those of the three Western powers (*Figure 1.1*). By the late 1940s those parts of the continent which had been liberated by the Red Army and subsequently occupied by the Soviets formed the Soviet Union's East European buffer against the West. They were in the process of being forged together in political, military and economic organizations in which the ultimate power was located outside their own territories. Their sovereignty in the Western sense of the word was effectively curtailed.

In the diverse lands to the west of this Iron Curtain there remained, however, some sixteen sovereign states on whose individual freedom of action there were no forms of mandatory external control. Since the sixteenth century no limitation on the absolute authority of states had ever been voluntarily accepted and, whatever its other merits may have been, this had hardly proved to be a satisfactory method for conducting intra-European relations. Peace on the continent had largely depended on the maintenace of some form of 'balance of power' among the most powerful states but when, as so often happened, this balance failed then war was the inevitable recourse. Underlying the carnage and destruction of the first half of the twentieth century had been the threat implied in German aggression to upset this precarious balance.

With the initial reinstatement of the system of sovereign states in the western part of the continent after World War II came the beginnings of a return to the mutual suspicions and mistrusts which had always been the seedbed of war. Antipathy was most strongly directed towards Germany, branded by common consensus as the principal aggressor state during both wars and, in the second, the convicted perpetrator of the most appalling criminal acts. In the wake of the war there was a widespread feeling of unwillingness to allow such a country ever again to resume its place as a great power in Europe. Although Germany had suffered the most crushing defeat it was remembered only too well that in 1918 her recovery from defeat had been as politically disastrous as it had been economically impressive. The factors underlying German strength had long been perceived as being primarily in her 'geology and human ecology'[4], and neither of these had been substantially altered by defeat. Her reserves of coal, lignite and minerals remained impressive, and her total population was scarcely less than that in 1939. The fear engendered by these statistics was greatest in Western Europe's old hegemonial power, France, which was preoccupied with the problem of finding a solution to this seemingly inevitable German strength. It had been the same in 1918, but by the 1930s France had been relegated to the humiliating position of watching helplessly from behind her Maginot Line[5] the re-emergence of that overwhelming German strength which in 1940 was to engineer her eclipse. The countervailing alliances which France had made with Britain and with certain East European states[6] had been decisively worsted, and had it not been for the unwilling intervention of the United States for a second time on the side of

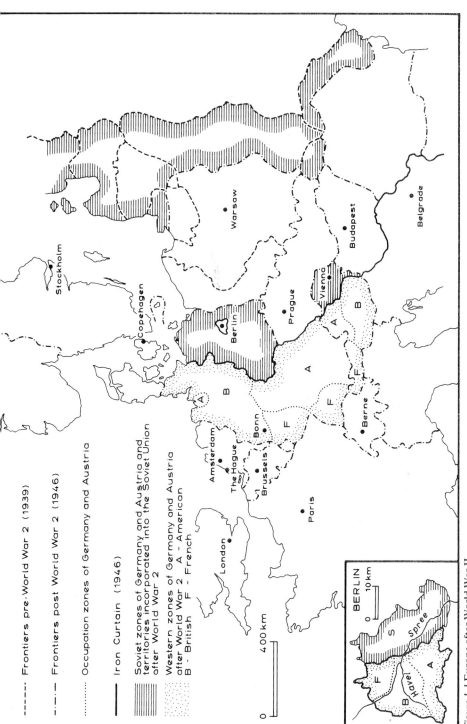

Frontiers pre-World War 2 (1939)

Frontiers post World War 2 (1946)

Occupation zones of Germany and Austria

Iron Curtain (1946)

Soviet zones of Germany and Austria and territories incorporated into the Soviet Union after World War 2

Western zones of Germany and Austria after World War 2   A - American
B - British   F - French

Stockholm
Copenhagen
Berlin
Warsaw
Prague
Vienna
Budapest
Belgrade
Berne
Bonn
Amsterdam
The Hague
Brussels
Paris
London

A
B
F

0   400 km

BERLIN
0   10 km
Havel
Spree
S
B
A
F

Figure 1.1 Europe after World War II

Western democracies, the eclipse would in all probability have proved to be total. Thus for the second time in a generation, Germany, uneasily balanced between maritime and continental Europe and divided by the increasingly impermeable Iron Curtain, appeared to be Europe's most pressing international problem.

In the mid-1940s three possible solutions to this problem were being canvassed by the Allies, these being 'pastoralization', division and external control. The idea of 'pastoralization' was found in its most extreme form in the Morgenthau Plan of 1944[7], and it entailed the de-industrialization of the country so as to remove the economic base necessary to any future aggressive expansion. The idea of division, which had long been attractive to France, entailed the re-partition of the country into small states similar to those which had existed in the early nineteenth century. It was envisaged that in this way the big bad gangster Reich, modelled on Prussia, would be replaced by 'good little Germanies', living as before in colourful and bucolic bliss and presenting no conceivable threat to Europe's international order. The third possible solution, that of permanent, or long-term, external control, required an international apparatus which would steer Germany's massive economic strength into the paths of peace.

Elements of each of these possible solutions were to be found in the regime imposed by Britain, France and the United States on the western part of Germany after 1945. The International Ruhr Authority[8] was given the task of regulating the country's output of heavy industrial goods. There was at first some dismantling and selling off of heavy industrial plant, especially that of the great 'barons' believed to have been closely associated with Nazi war crimes. Division was also implicit in the three zones of occupation, each of which was at first administered according to the ideas of the particular occupying power, while in overall charge of the affairs of the defeated country there was the four-power Allied Control Commission, the major task of which became the regulating of inter-zonal contacts. However, all these measures were seen by the occupiers as essentially temporary until a four-power peace treaty could resurrect a German state acceptable to the victors.

In the absence of an early solution, an effort was made to strengthen Allied power. The Treaty of Dunkirk set a seal on the Anglo–French alliance, and this was followed in 1948 by the Brussels Treaty, which was signed by Britain, France and the three countries of Benelux. Each of these five undertook to go to the aid of any one of their number which became the object of an armed attack in Europe by a third country. It also set up machinery for coordinating foreign policies and for cooperating in a wide range of economic, social and cultural fields. This treaty was a belated attempt to bind together the collective strength of the Western democracies in a way which, had it then been possible, would have been eminently suited to the international conditions prevailing in 1939. In the meantime the German horse had bolted, and the treaty did not solve the problem of what to do about it.

At the same time on a larger geographical stage the process of binding the United States into a peacetime alliance with her former wartime partners was taking place. At first this had little appeal in America, and was at variance with the traditional American freedom from 'foreign entanglements' for which there was a historic mistrust, especially in regard to Europe. However, the dangers inherent in the solidification of Soviet influence in the eastern part of the continent for an economically weak, politically fragmented and militarily vulnerable western periphery produced a rapid turnround in the Truman administration's thinking during the latter part of 1947. This change of attitude was strongly encouraged by Britain which, seeing her world power slipping away from her, felt acutely the need of American support to bolster the maritime world. So, following the proclamation of the Truman Doctrine[9], the United States was persuaded to don the neo-imperial mantle and become the centre of a new Atlantic system. George Marshall, the American Secretary of State, proposed a massive aid programme for Europe, conditional upon the Europeans being able to establish a suitable international organization to handle it. At a conference called jointly by Britain and France this arrangement was accepted by sixteen non-Communist European states[10], and in 1948 the Organization for European Economic Cooperation (OEEC) came into being. Between then and 1952 OEEC disbursed American aid to the value of some $17 000 million, which helped to put the economies of the countries of Western Europe on a much firmer footing. In 1949 this massive transfer of funds was complemented by the signature of the Treaty of Washington, which established the North Atlantic Treaty Organization. The initial signatories were the United States, Canada, Britain, France, Belgium, the Netherlands, Italy, Denmark, Norway, Iceland and Portugal. Greece and Turkey joined in 1952 and the German Federal Republic in 1955[11]. The Treaty had many provisions, but basically the members all agreed to provide mutual assistance should one of their number be attacked in the North Atlantic area. The undisputed centre of power in this Atlantic alliance was the United States, which now became not just the 'arsenal of democracy' as in World War II but its banker, quartermaster and commanding officer as well. America was persuaded to undertake this course of action because of her increasing preoccupation, from 1947 on, with the danger of possible further Soviet expansion coupled with subversive Communist penetration into the Western world. From her perceived position in the centre of the Western system America came to regard maritime Europe, and especially those parts adjacent to the Iron Curtain, as a glacis in the defence of the West and especially of 'fortress America'.

Thus before 1950 there were in maritime Europe two principal levels of international system. There was first the Brussels Treaty organization, which was directed principally to the problem of Germany and which sought to deal with it through a combination of collective strength and measures to prevent a resurgence of German power. The second was the Atlantic Alliance, which was directed squarely against the Soviet Union and for which the German question was a secondary consideration. While in certain ways the two systems were mutually reinforcing, it became clear that there were certain fundamental incompatibilities. To the continental Europeans the 'German trees' were, in Mollet's phrase, more important than the 'Russian forest' since they were much closer. The British perception had from the beginning been closer to that of the Americans. The problem of compatibility between the two views came to the fore when the United States made it clear that she wished to achieve the rapid rehabilitation of Germany. This demand became more insistent after the outbreak of the Korean War in June 1950 and the imperative need for Germany to make a positive contribution to the Western Alliance.

Neither 'pastoralization', division nor international control had ever been considered by the Anglo–Americans as permanent solutions to the German problem. France had, after 1945, wished to explore these possibilities further, but both Britain and America, remembering the tragic results of their German policy after World War I, tended to discourage French ideas. France, the weaker partner at the time, was in no position to take an independent line from that of her powerful allies. Although suspicious of *les anglo-saxons* she knew well enough that, for the time being, they were her only effective guarantors. The Anglo–American zones were merged to create 'Bizonia', and it was not long before France was forced to follow suit. In 1949 the foundations of the German Federal Republic were laid when a government was installed having authority over all three Western zones. The economic strength of the new state was steadily increasing and the Americans considered this as a desirable development to be encouraged and, if possible, speeded up. This situation did not in any way allay French fears about the nature of the emerging West German state, but the French government was conscious of the limitations which its weakness placed upon its ability to influence the course of events.

Within this uneasy situation, a third line of action began now to play an increasing role. This was the resuscitation of the idea of some sort of federal union of the European states. In 1947 the European Movement had sponsored the Hague Conference, which had brought together representatives from most of Europe's democratic states. At this Conference the decision was made to set up a European parliament, to be called the Council of Europe, which would assemble in the war-torn city of Strasbourg on the Rhine. The first meeting of the Council took place in the autumn of 1949 and there was much initial enthusiasm for the establishment of the institutions for a European government. However, by the beginning of 1950 much of the early euphoria had been dissipated and the deliberations had become deadlocked. There was a seemingly irreconcilable divergence of views between those who wished to press ahead without delay with the creation of a federal government having supranational powers and those who wished rather to continue to operate within the traditional international framework. The French were broadly in favour of moving towards federalism while the British would have nothing to do with this approach: not for the first time, a crack appeared in the *entente cordiale*.

It was in this atmosphere of deadlock in Europe, coupled with mounting pressure from the United States, that the French Foreign Minister addressed his proposals to Germany for the integration of the heavy industries of the two countries. The Schuman Declaration of 9 May 1950 was, in fact, almost entirely the work of Jean Monnet and his colleagues at the French *Commissariat du Plan*. Monnet, a distinguished civil servant and one-time Assistant Secretary-General to the League of Nations, had become increasingly fearful as he saw French policy towards Germany begin to slip back into its old ways, ready to repeat all the errors, as he saw them, of the past. He was convinced that the problem posed by Germany's seemingly inevitable industrial pre-eminence and the fears which this naturally produced in France needed to be tackled in a new way. He had watched successive French governments being 'locked into the post-war situation' and wedded to traditional solutions which were clearly unacceptable to the country's principal allies. It was imperative to break fresh ground, and this could only be achieved, as Monnet saw it, through a sublimation of national self-interest. This had to be done initially by the exercise of joint sovereignty over resources using entirely new international frameworks of control. These were enshrined in the Schuman Declaration:

> Europe will not be built all at once, or through a single comprehensive plan. It will be built through concrete achievements, which will first create a *de facto* solidarity. The comity of European nations requires that the rivalry of France and Germany should be eliminated. Action should therefore first be concentrated on France and Germany. The French government proposes immediate action on a limited but decisive point: my government proposes to place the whole of the production of coal and steel in France and Germany under a common high authority in an organization open to the participation of the other countries of Europe. The pooling of the production of coal and steel will immediately establish a common basis for economic development.

As Schuman put it, it was time for empty words to be replaced by 'a bold act, a constructive act'. The proposals were immediately accepted by the fledgling German Federal Republic as a basis for negotiation. Italy and the three Benelux countries also gave notice that they were in favour but Britain, whose participation was at first considered by Monnet to be absolutely essential, stood aloof. She was, after all, still Europe's strongest country, one of the 'Big Three', and the cultivation of the Empire–Commonwealth was widely regarded as being the country's true destiny. British negativeness acted as a discouragement to many countries, but this did not prevent the 'inner six' from going ahead (*Figure 1.2*). In April 1951 came the signature of the Treaty of Paris establishing a European Coal and Steel Community. It was to have control over intra-Community trade in coal, iron, steel, lignite and scrap metals. Tariff and other internal restrictions on free trade in these commodities were to be removed, fair competition to be ensured and aid from ECSC funds to be provided to help particular industries, regions and groups of workers to adjust to the new conditions. The preamble to the Treaty stated that this was not seen simply as an end in itself but as a basis for wider cooperation. The participating countries were

> Resolved to substitute for age-old rivalries the merging of their essential interests: to create, by establishing an economic community, the basis for a broader and deeper community among peoples long divided by bloody conflicts and to lay the foundations for institutions which will give direction to a destiny henceforth shared.

The ECSC started work in 1952. Its headquarters were in Luxembourg and its controlling body was the High Authority, of which the first president was, appropriately enough, Jean Monnet. In addition, a Council of Ministers was to represent national governments, a Court to judge in

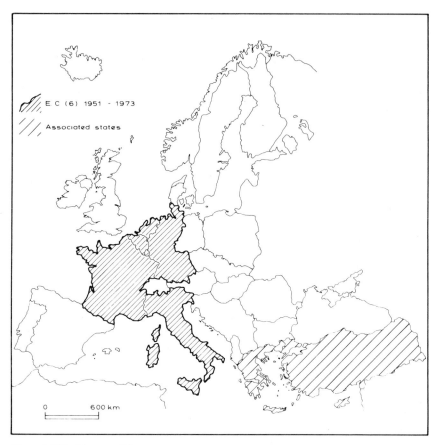

E C (6) 1951 - 1973

Associated states

0   600 km

Figure 1.2 The Europe of Six

Community disputes and a Common Assembly of parliamentarians to monitor progress and pass judgement on it.

The twin breakthroughs represented by ECSC were the creating of a supranational organization with its own powers and sanctions and the bridging of the great divide between the belligerents of World War II. Its success engendered such enthusiasm that it was followed by similarly conceived schemes covering other aspects of international affairs. The most significant of these was the 'Pleven Plan' for the establishment of a defence community possessing its own armed forces. A treaty establishing this European Defence Community was duly signed but, while it was ratified by five of the legislatures, the French National Assembly finally rejected it in 1954. France, after stepping into the unknown with Schuman's 'bold act', began to fear the possible consequences of further military cooperation with her muscular neighbour across the Rhine. A defence community as a possible 'cage for the German tiger' took on the appearance to many Frenchmen of a cage in which the Gallic cock would also be incarcerated. The participation of the Benelux countries and Italy were not sufficiently reassuring, and the integrative process ground to a halt with only the limited, although successful, ECSC to its credit.

This self-induced failure also posed a problem for the granting of full sovereignty to the German Federal Republic. This had been made conditional upon the implementation of EDC, and the new *wehrmacht* was to be integrated immediately into its command structure. A solution was found by a retreat into the traditional alliance system with the establishment of a Western European Union. This replaced the Brussels Treaty, was joined by Germany and incorporated a reinforced British military guarantee to Europe.

This failure to extend the area of functional cooperation demonstrated that the national hackles were likely to be raised less by economic than by political or military questions. In 1955 a conference of the foreign ministers of the Six at Messina produced an agreement to commence fresh advances in the building of Europe, and the communiqué stated that this should again take place in the economic sphere. A committee under the chairmanship of the Belgian Foreign Minister, Paul Spaak, advocated the setting up of a full customs union rather than simply a free trade area[12]. Like the Schuman Declaration of six years earlier, the Spaak Report was accepted by the governments of the Six as a basis for further negotiation. Although present at certain sessions as an observer, Britain again declined the profferred invitation to participate. Consequently a conference of the Six was convened in Rome in January 1957 and in March the two Treaties of Rome were signed: they established the European Economic Community and the European Atomic Energy Community. The first of these set a ten-year timetable for the creation of a full customs union, with a special policy to be worked out to take into account the problems facing Europe's agriculture. It was agreed that colonial and mandated territories of member states should have an association agreement and that direct Community aid should be provided for them. The EEC treaty also contained provisions for policies in the fields of regional development, social affairs, industrial restructuring and currency reform. EAEC (Euratom) had the task of developing the peaceful uses of nuclear energy, which was believed to hold out great promise for the future.

The British government felt in 1957, as it had felt in 1950, that membership was not compatible with the country's other international commitments. Despite the considerable diminution in her international position in the previous ten years, Britain still thought in global rather than in regional terms, and envisaged the Commonwealth as the vehicle for her continuing world role. The Commonwealth was, in the Churchillian imperial view, the 'first circle' of British interests, and Europe was relegated to the third behind the United States[13]. In the middle 1950s Europe was still regarded as being a relative backwater, albeit a troublesome one, in so far as major British interests were concerned. However, by the late 1950s it was coming to be increasingly realized that it was desirable to seek some positive trade arrangement with Europe, and this led in 1959 to the Stockholm Agreements establishing the European Free Trade Association. The members were Denmark, Norway, Sweden, Switzerland, Austria, Portugal and Britain. These 'outer seven' were countries which had found it neither possible nor relevant to participate in the closer Community arrangements. EFTA was a much looser grouping than the EC, but its arrival produced an economic split of maritime Europe throughout the 1960s.

The two new Communities came into being in 1958, with their headquarters at Brussels. The executive body of each was a Commission, initially of nine members, and the other institutions of ECSC, the Council, the Court and the Common Assembly, also acted for the new Communities. Progress in establishing the customs union was more rapid than had been thought possible, and it came into full operation in 1966, two years ahead of schedule. Like ECSC before it, it was at first seen as one link in a longer chain of cooperation, while by the early 1960s it had become a great success in its own right. It came into being at the beginning of post-war Europe's age of 'economic miracles', during which growth and prosperity increased rapidly. A large share of the credit for this success was claimed by the protagonists of the Communities. Their internationalist, liberal and free trade policies stood out in such stark contrast to the nationalistic autarchy which had prevailed a quarter of a century earlier, and which had been associated with such unmitigated disaster, political as well as economic. Britain's international economic position was, by contrast, far less buoyant, and its further deterioration was the background to the first British application to join the EC in 1961. However, times had changed, and a knock from across the Channel no longer guaranteed the opening of doors in Europe. France's tentative step into the unknown a decade earlier had apparently paid off. There was a new self-confidence, and the Anglo-Saxon crutch was less needed. Beside, since 1958 the country had been ruled by the nationalist and authoritarian government of General de Gaulle, which was displaying a measure of xenophobia towards the Anglo-Saxon powers. In January 1963 the French vetoed British membership after eighteen months of negotiations, the reason given being that Britain was not 'European' enough. It is now questionable to what extent de Gaulle's France was itself actually much more 'European' in this implied sense. The Community's aspirations had been at one stage dubbed by de Gaulle as being 'ill-founded Utopian myths'[14], and the Commission dismissed as a 'méli-mélo'. It appears rather more likely that, with the passing of the French dream of a 'blood and sand' empire in Africa, there appeared a new Gaullist vision of a constellation of European states with France as *primus inter pares*. If de Gaulle could not be a latter-day Marshal Lyautey, he could at least endeavour to become a new Charlemagne[15]. At all events, he considered one cock and five hens to be at this time quite enough for the European barnyard.

It was not until 1973, four years after the departure of de Gaulle from the scene, that Britain finally became a member of the EC (*Figure 1.3*). With her world trade shrunk, her empire gone and many of her basic industries in a terminal condition, this shabby vestige of the global power which had said 'no' so firmly a quarter of a century earlier was no longer perceived as a threat to the French idea of Europe. In any case, de Gaulle's more pedestrian successors appeared prepared to accept a less pre-eminent role for their country. The smarting memory of *le débâcle* of 1940, which had so strongly affected de Gaulle and many of his age group, was dimmed for a younger generation, born since World War II, by the tangible if prosaic advantages of economic success in a Europe at peace. *La gloire* was out of fashion, as was empire-building, and had been replaced by economic growth and material prosperity, the prospects for which still seemed in the

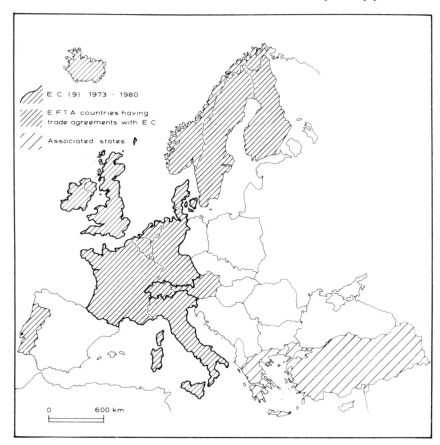

Figure 1.3 The Europe of Nine

early 1970s to be endless. Denmark and Ireland, both closely tied economically to Britain, also joined the Communities in 1973, and eight years later in 1981 Greece became the tenth member (*Figure 1.4*).

The way in which, by the early 1970s, the European Communities came to be associated with a state of peace and economic prosperity in Europe appeared to vindicate the faith which had been held in the value of functional economic cooperation as a catalyst for a more general progress towards unity. The EC had emerged out of the clear inadequacies of traditionally conceived alliances to tackle the post-1945 situation. Yet this same functional approach had failed when the attempt had been made to apply it to non-economic areas. The functionalist claim that integration in one limited area can spill over into others was, however, substantiated by the extent to which Community activity had by the 1970s moved into new areas only vaguely envisaged in the founding treaties. Despite its many problems it continued to display an evolutionary dynamism which has been less evident in other international systems.

In the early 1950s there were in maritime Europe five major international systems, and the protagonists of each were engaged in demonstrating

E C (10)

E F.T.A. countries having
trade agreements with E C.

Associated states

0   600 km

Figure 1.4 The Europe of Ten

their particular merits in meeting the needs of the times. These systems
were the Brussels Treaty Organization, the Atlantic Alliance, the Council
of Europe, the Community (ECSC) and, finally, the states themselves as a
form of international system. Each of these tended to have its own
principal objectives, but each inherently possessed the possibilities for
extension into a more total and comprehensive system. By the early 1980s,
thirty years later, the positions of each of the five had considerably altered.
The Brussels Treaty Organization was subsumed in 1955 into the Western
European Union, which has maintained no more than a vestigial existence,
and the Council of Europe, upon which great hopes had been pinned by
the federalists, remained largely an international forum. The other three
were the real survivors, and had become apexes of the triangle of
international power in Europe (*Figure 1.5*). The Atlantic Alliance remains
basically for defence: the activities of the Communities continue to operate
principally in the economic sphere while the states are still the political
decision-makers and retain effective vetoes on their participation in
international action. However, there are – in many ways intentionally –
many grey areas of competence and the relative positions and functions of
the three have been steadily, if imperceptibly, changing.

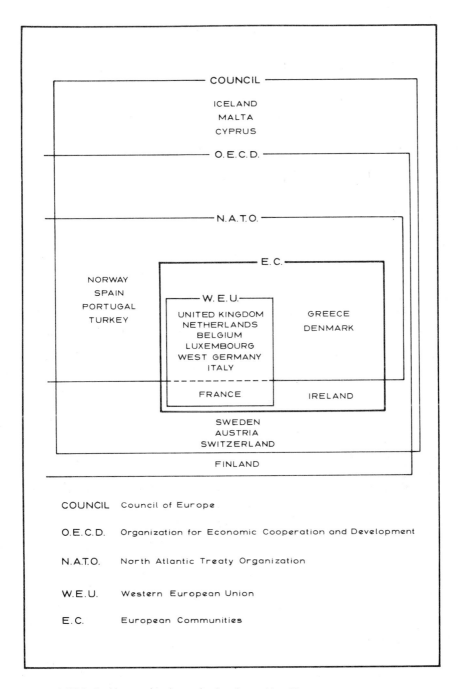

Figure 1.5 Principal international organizations in maritime Europe

The Atlantic Alliance, although it has gained four new members since being set up in 1949, has not substantially changed its overall role. The states, although clearly inadequate as the sovereign units of political organization, have been able to maintain and even in some ways enhance their positions as repositories of final authority. Underlying this has been the continued mass appeal of nationalism and the failure of wider loyalties to supplant this. Many governments have fostered and encouraged this for the purpose of justifying the maintenance of power in their own hands. In spite of this, the Communities have proved to be the most dynamic in the process of adaptation to new conditions. The 1950s preoccupation with peace, reconciliation and the international control of industrial power gave place in the new conditions of the 1960s to the achievement of economic prosperity through wide-ranging measures of economic integration. Subsequently questions of regional imbalance, energy, environmental protection, foreign policy and world trade have become important, and new strategies have been developed in these fields. Such are the linkages which exist among the various forms of functional cooperation in the international sphere.

Ever since the decline of Christendom and the crystallization of the territorial states there has been a strand of concern with the recreation of the lost unity of the past. They range from the Duc de Sully's *Grand Dessein* in the seventeenth century to the Briand Plan of the inter-war years. However, over this long period no limitation was ever accepted voluntarily on the absolute authority of the state over its own affairs until the Schuman Plan rapidly began the transformation of hopes into realities. The time of the idea of Europe appeared to have at last come.

The particular propitiousness of the post-war period for the transformation of at least some internationalist ideas into reality has been explained in various ways. The essential elements in world geopolitical change after 1945 as it affected maritime Europe were the emergence of the United States and the Soviet Union as the centres of real world power and, at the same time, the rapid waning of the Eurocentric global empires. Within a decade of the emergence of the Americans and the Soviets from their generation of self-imposed isolation, the Eurocentric world had given place to a bi-polar one. In Galtung's words.

> The entry of the Soviet Union and the United States [into World War II] in 1941 . . . spelt the defeat not only of Germany, but for Europe also. Europe from Brest (Brittany) to Brest (Litovsk) was no longer able to handle her own affairs. Europe as such was defeated by the war, not only Germany.[16]

Most threatening to European independence in those years appeared to be the Soviet Union. Militarily powerful, occupying entrenched positions in the heart of Europe and seemingly imbued with a crusading zest, this enigmatic Eurasian state is thought by many to have been the principal external catalyst to unity. As Lukacs put it,

> The grim armed mass of pre-Asian Russians, camped and settled across the middle of Europe, was the most powerful incentive of the new West European order that was constructed after the war.[17]

While the European countries were ~~thus~~ impelled to take collective action to rectify their state of weakness, it was also ~~glaringly~~ apparent that the system of nation states had failed to achieve a stable peace and to secure the level of life which might have been expected from the continent's wealth. The system, or rather the lack of it, had presided over the killing of the equivalent of the total population of one large European power during the previous half-century and had brought the continent near to irreversible ruin. The lessons of the retreats from internationalism to nationalism after previous wars could no longer be ignored. In 1950 it was looking as though not just France but much of maritime Europe was about to return to its old ways again, having, like the Bourbons before it, learnt nothing and forgotten nothing.

Both wars were very much in the memories of those at the helm in the countries of Europe during the 1950s, and many had personal experience of their horrors. Many more had been associated with the resistance movements of World War II, and in those dark times the ideal of a unified Europe after the war had given hope for an end to the periodic ritual of internecine blood-letting. To many such leaders the states appeared to be inherently unsatisfactory clay for the building of a more enduring European order. They had been tried and found wanting in this respect over and over again. Community-style internationalism was thus also a response to a growing sense of unease about the nature of the 'nation state' and its ability to produce a better order of things. It was also a time when the whole of maritime Europe looked like being relegated to the role of the glacis of an American-dominated Atlantic system. The problem of international order in Europe, centring on the German question, now appeared to be on a collision course with the issues arising from the growing confrontation of the superpowers. It was the necessity to find an immediate solution to this dichotomy which impelled six of the European states to break through the international thought-barrier into a new form of cooperation which within a few years was to change the course of events. It was what Jean Monnet had referred to as 'a breach in the ramparts of sovereignty which will be narrow enough to secure consent, but deep enough to open the way towards the unity that is essential to peace'[18]. It entailed the gradual shift of power over affairs to the institutions of the Community, a process which, if continued, would make a future war, in the words of the Schuman Declaration, 'not only unthinkable but materially impossible'. It was also assumed that as power slipped away from the states, their power to influence events would also become progressively less.

The advantages of economic cooperation and of increased international strength through unity were accepted gradually after the initial establishment of the three Communities. They had not themselves been the *prima mobile* but rather constituted part of the range of effects, covering all aspects of international action, which resulted from the establishment of the EC. It was also demonstrated that the 'Community method' is capable of being used in any international situation, and this makes it inherently so different from the 'classical method' of mono-functional alliance. The capacity for adaptation had resulted in its evolution as the conditions and policies which originally gave birth to it were succeeded by others of a radically different character.

The Community has thus been powerfully moulded by the imperatives of history, but it also has its geographical imperatives firmly grounded in the nature of the territory of maritime Europe, and especially that of its most centrally placed regions. It was this territory which contributed to producing the problems, but which subsequently also suggested the possibilities for their resolution.

Notes

1. The Yalta Conference took place in February 1945 and the Potsdam Conference in July–August 1945. In both of them the only participants were the representatives of the 'Big Three' victorious powers. On Churchill's insistence it was agreed that France should also be given a zone in post-war Germany and be involved in the administration of the defeated country. France was thus implicitly recognized as one of the 'Big Four' from then on

2. This was the line proposed by Great Britain in 1920 as the definitive Polish–Russian frontier. It was named after Lord Curzon, the British Foreign Secretary at the time. It follows roughly the ethnic divide between the Poles on one side and the Ukrainians and White Russians on the other. While it was not accepted at the time, the Soviet Union found it to her advantage to propose it to the Polish government as their mutual frontier in 1945. In view of the change in the balance of power it was then accepted by Poland, and Britain found it difficult to find reasons for opposing it.

3. This phrase was made famous by Churchill in a speech delivered at Fulton, Missouri, in March 1946. It had previously been used by Joseph Goebbels, Nazi propaganda minister, and by Count Schwerin von Krosigk, a minister in the last government of the Third Reich. Both appear to have foreseen, with a clarity perhaps stemming from the German geopolitical tradition, the forthcoming division of Europe into two hostile camps

4. D. W. Brogan, *The French Nation from Napoleon to Pétain*, London, 1957

5. Massive fortified frontier line facing Germany, named after André Maginot, the French Minister of War. It extended 200 km from the Swiss frontier as far as Luxembourg, but it was around its northern flank that the German Panzers broke through in May 1940

6. France attempted to establish a system of alliances between herself and the newly established countries of eastern Europe after 1918. Policy differences made this an increasingly difficult task, and in 1938 France weakly acquiesced in the dismemberment of her ally Czechoslovakia (the Munich Crisis). By 1939 all that remained was the Anglo–French guarantee to Poland which was to trigger off World War II

7. Named after Henry Morgenthau, US Secretary to the Treasury, who in 1944 proposed the de-industrialization of Germany after the war in order to ensure that the country would never again be in a position to make war on its neighbours. It was at first accepted by the British and American governments, but was soon rejected as being quite impracticable

8. Set up in 1949 for the purpose of controlling and monitoring the growth of heavy industry in this region following the economic merger of the three Western zones and the establishment of a federal authority in Bonn

9. The Truman Doctrine, named after President Harry S. Truman, was enunciated in an address to Congress in March 1947. It pledged American support for 'free peoples who are resisting attempted subjugation by armed minorities or by outside pressures'. Prompted by the apparent dangers to the West of the civil war in Greece between the government and the Communists, it marked a complete change in American post-war policy

10. The initial offer of aid was made to all the countries of Europe. The Soviet Union found itself unable to accept the internationalist approach insisted upon by the Americans and so withdrew from further participation

11. Spain became the sixteenth member of the Alliance in 1982

12. The idea of a free trade area was proposed as an alternative by Britain. While this would have resulted in the removal of internal trade restrictions, it would have been left to individual countries to determine their own external trade policies. This would have suited Britain far better, since it would not have interfered with her system of 'imperial preference'. Negotiations on this basis were entered into between the 'Six' and Britain, but they came to nothing

13. 'The first circle for us is naturally the British Commonwealth and Empire, with all that it comprises. Then there is also the English-speaking world in which we, Canada and the other dominions play so important a part. And finally there is united Europe'. Speech by Winston Churchill in the House of Commons, 27 June 1950
14. President de Gaulle said at his press conference on 9 September 1965 that France would return to the Common Market when 'people are ready to have done with the pretensions which ill-founded utopian myths raise up against common sense and reality'
15. In 1950 de Gaulle ('like the Chorus in some Greek tragedy', as Monnet saw it) had commented on the Schuman Plan: 'If one were not constrained to look at matters coolly, one would be dazzled by the prospect of what could be achieved by a combination of German and French strength, the latter embracing also Africa . . . Altogether it would mean giving modern economic, social, strategic and cultural shape to the work of the Emperor Charlemagne.' Quoted in Jean Monnet, *Memoirs*, London, 1978
16. J. Galtung, *The European Community: A Superpower in the Making*, London, 1973
17. J. Lukacs, *Decline and Rise of Europe*, Westport, 1976
18. J. Monnet, op. cit.

Chapter 2

The member states: spatial features and contemporary change

In order to arrive at some understanding of the territorial *raison d'être* underlying the European Community it is first necessary to examine the geopolitical structures of the units of which it is composed. It is particularly important to understand the situation around the middle of the twentieth century at the time of the establishment of the first of the Communities.

It was France which had taken the initiative in 1950 and it was here that the Community idea was carefully nurtured. At the time it was the only West European power with both the strength and the will to pursue it, and it became a kind of sublimation of French foreign policy over the previous thirty years.

France is a very old state, tracing its origins back to the Empire of Charlemagne in the ninth century. The historic core area of the feudal French state was the Paris–Orléans area, home of the Capet dynasty, and from there control extended in medieval times over the rich and fertile lands of the Paris basin. There was subsequently further extension through the Poitou gap into the Aquitaine basin and eastwards to Burgundy and the Rhône valley. From then on there was a gradual eastwards movement of the frontiers, by the seventeenth century reaching the Rhine and the Alps, so forming the outlines of the French 'hexagon', which was subsequently to play so important a part in French geopolitical mythology. It also engendered that idea of 'natural frontiers' which was to play a significant part in French international thinking during its age of pre-eminence in the seventeenth and eighteenth centuries. The frontiers were well defined and readily defensible in the east, south-east and south, but the north-eastern frontier was part of the North European plain, and there was nothing very 'natural' about it[1]. An attempt was made to push the frontier eastwards to the Rhine, but this was blocked by successive coalitions made up of France's neighbours and led by the Netherlands and England. The search for security, closely associated with a forward policy on the eastern frontier, remained a continuing cause of conflict with the neighbouring states of the Rhinelands, and this aggressive frontier policy culminated in the Revolutionary and Napoleonic Wars. It was eventually curtailed by the massive defeats inflicted on France in the early nineteenth century by the coalitions of European powers, and it was replaced by a policy of holding the frontiers stemming from that defensive psychology which culminated in the Maginot Line of the 1930s and the crushing defeat by Germany in 1940.

Underlying the change in French psychology from aggressive to defensive state was the reduction in relative physical strength. In the eighteenth century France had been the most powerful state in Europe, as judged by the combined criteria of size of territory, population and both agricultural and industrial production. This enabled the maintenance of a massive military establishment to further the territorial ambitions of her rulers. However, from the end of the eighteenth century this situation had begun to change. Population and production increases were slower than those of neighbouring countries. The twenty-five years of revolution and war which began in 1789 bled the country white, and subsequently British industrial innovation affected France much less than her eastern neighbours into which advanced technology from Britain was first disseminated. Following defeat in the Franco–Prussian War of 1871, Alsace and eastern Lorraine were annexed by the new German Empire, and this lost France resources of Jurassic iron ore which would have proved valuable in industrial development. France was now forced to bolster her position by entering into an alliance with Russia in 1891 and the *entente cordiale* with Britain in 1904. After World War I she tried to construct an alliance system in eastern Europe, but her position had so far deteriorated by 1940 that her defeat by the numerically inferior German forces took a mere six weeks.

With an area of 550 000 km^2 France is more than twice the size of the United Kingdom and is the largest country in Western Europe (*Table 2.1*).

TABLE 2.1. Extent, population and production of the member countries of the European Communities

	Area (000 km^2)	Population (millions)	Energy production (million tonnes oil equivalent)	Energy consumption (million tonnes oil equivalent)	GDP (mrd ECU)
West Germany	61.4	248.6	121.9	281.8	592.1
France	53.5	544.0	37.7	185.3	469.4
Italy	56.9	301.3	18.3	134.1	283.7
Netherlands	14.0	41.2	73.6	67.6	108.8
Belgium	9.8	30.5	6.8	48.5	79.0
Luxembourg	0.4	2.6	–	3.8	3.0
United Kingdom	55.9	244.1	192.6	219.8	319.9
Ireland	3.4	70.3	1.1	8.4	10.8
Denmark	5.1	43.1	0.4	20.3	48.3
Greece	9.4	132.0	3.2	15.4	28.0

Source: EC Statistical Office, Luxembourg, 1981

However, her population after World War II was just over 40 millions, far less than the other major West European countries. Her density of population of 75 per km^2 contrasted with West Germany's of over 200 and the countries of Benelux with over 300. This made France one of the more lightly populated countries in Western Europe. Just over one-third of the labour force was still gaining its living by working on the land, while only

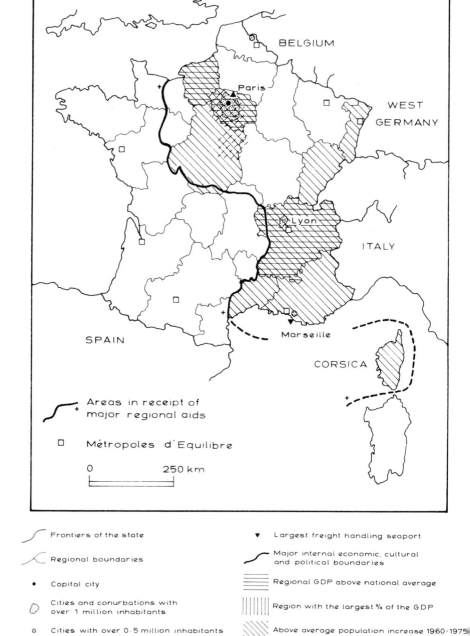

BELGIUM

WEST GERMANY

Paris

Lyon

ITALY

Marseille

SPAIN

CORSICA

⌒✝ Areas in receipt of
   major regional aids

☐ Métropoles d'Equilibre

0   250 km

Frontiers of the state

Regional boundaries

• Capital city

Cities and conurbations with
over 1 million inhabitants

○ Cities with over 0·5 million inhabitants

▲ Principal national airport

▼ Largest freight handling seaport

Major internal economic, cultural
and political boundaries

Regional GDP above national average

Region with the largest % of the GDP

Above average population increase 1960-1975

Historic core area of the state

Figure 2.1 The spatial structure of France

about the same number were working in industry. This gave France one of the highest proportions of the labour force in agriculture and lowest in industry in the whole of Western Europe, and these figures indicate the relative backwardness and under-industrialization of the country. At a time when coal and steel production were still prime indicators of national strength, France's position was also a weak one. Coal output of some 50 million tons was only a quarter that of Britain, and steel production was little more than a half of the British total. These were inadequate to supply needs, and there was little energy forthcoming from other indigenous sources at the time.

Levels of urbanization in France were also low by the standards of neighbouring countries, and the census of 1946 showed only three cities with populations of over half a million each. The outstanding exception to this was, of course, the capital, which had a population of 2.7 millions and there was an almost equal number in the *auréole* of satellite towns. This demographic pre-eminence was repeated in most other aspects of the national life. France had been run as a highly centralized state for centuries, and by the middle of the twentieth century the dominance of the capital city in virtually every sphere of the national life was almost total. The dichotomy of 'Paris and the provinces', the head and the body, had led to cynical comments that France had become merely a suburb of Paris. J.-F. Gravier wrote that Paris had 'devoured the provinces', implying that the historic vitality of this large and diverse land had been emasculated by its predatory capital city[1]. France had become a manifestation of the spatial implications of Hobbes' Leviathan, and the regional inequalities which may result from it. However, in spite of this dominance, the importance of physical resources had produced a concentration of heavy industry in the resource-rich north and east, where most of the coal and iron is to be found. These areas were the only significant counterweights to what would otherwise have been the total dominance of Paris. Thus in overall economic terms the country's north-east quadrant – Paris/Nord/Lorraine – was pre-eminent, while the south and west remained agrarian and relatively backward. This geographical distribution of activity was geopolitically a most unfortunate one, since the country's centre of gravity was in close juxtaposition to what, since the seventeenth century, had proved to be the most vulnerable frontier[2]. For this reason, attempts had been made to encourage industrial relocation into safer regions nearer the geographical centre of the country, and especially to the Massif Central, with its own small coalfields. However, this had not fundamentally altered that spatial pattern which had placed the country's centre of gravity so firmly in the north-east.

The country to which France tentatively put out the hand of friendship in the 'bold act' of 1950 was the new West Germany, just emerging out of the three Western zones and in 1954 to become fully sovereign as the German Federal Republic. France was making an attempt to break the cycle of wars between the two countries which dated, at least in its modern manifestation, from 1871. She was also fearful of being unable in any other way to control her powerful and aggressive eastern neighbour.

Germany was indeed in geopolitical terms a very different sort of state from herself. Until the early nineteenth century the territory which had become the Federal Republic consisted of a large number of small states still loosely grouped together within the Holy Roman Empire. It was not until 1871 that the German Empire was proclaimed at Versailles, with the Prussian king as the new emperor and Austria and the Hapsburgs excluded. Within a quarter of a century the German Empire had gained political and economic pre-eminence on the continent of Europe, a pre-eminence which became a bid for hegemony in the first half of the twentieth century. Although the monochrome of the political map gave, as always, the impression of internal homogeneity, Germany remained a country of considerable diversity, its only real bond being the German language. Geopolitically it was divided into two quite distinct parts. In the east lay Prussia, the mark state which had already risen to become one of Europe's great powers before the new Germany had coalesced around it. It had always been physically poor, a land of 'sour sandy soils'[3], largely agricultural and, situated as it was in the middle of the North European Plain, territorially ill-defined. This had given rise to Bismarck's assertion that 'Prussia's frontiers are its armies'. Its government was centralized, authoritarian and militaristic, drawing its strength from the junker class of large landowning families. It had from early times developed an aggressive expansionist ethos which had led inexorably to the creation of that united Germany in which it played a major role. In contrast the western part of the country, centring on the Rhine basin, had consisted historically of a large number of states and free cities. Its wealth owed much to the strength of its commerce and industry, and this was reflected in the flourishing of large and prosperous cities. The unifying bond between these two disparate areas was the German language, which had become from the early nineteenth century the focus of a strident German nationalism. The new entity's formidable strength came from the fusing of the statist and military traditions of the east with the economic power of the west. This power was further enhanced in the late nineteenth century by the growth of Europe's largest iron and steel industry, founded on the coal and iron deposits with which the new state was so well endowed. It was especially concentrated on the massive Ruhr coalfield and its associated river and canal systems.

Physically the German state was in many ways a macrocosm of Prussia, a slice through the centre of Europe from the sea to the Alps, but with ill-defined frontiers to east and west. Traditional Prussian military ideas, such as the country's real frontiers being its armies and attack being the best form of defence, appeared eminently applicable to Germany as a whole. This was the background to that muscular foreign policy, sustained by the power of its 'geology and human ecology' and encouraged by the fact that France's grip was weakening. By the early 1900s Germany's neighbours had become fearful of what they judged to be her hegemonial ambitions, ambitions which were eventually to be frustrated only by the intervention of the two peripheral great powers. Her strength, although great by European standards, was not sufficient to enable her to successfully take on the extra-European world as well. This was demonstrated in two world wars, and the German state, which was drastically pruned back in 1918, was cut in two after the defeat of 1945.

The new West German state which began to emerge out of the ruins of the Third Reich in 1949 had only half the area of the Germany of 1937, but

possessed three quarters of its population. This situation resulted largely from the expulsion and flight of Germans westwards from the 'lost lands' in the east and from the Soviet zone. This additional labour provided a resource which, added to all the others, stimulated the recovery of the country from the destruction of war. Coal output in 1950 had reached 119 million tons, over twice that of France, and steel production was 12 million tons. Nearly a half of the total labour force was in industry and only 15 per cent in agriculture, half the French proportion.

As to the character of the internal spatial structure, the contrast with France could not have been more striking. Now that Berlin, a city of 4 million people in 1939, was in the Soviet zone and under four-power control, the country had no dominating capital of the 'Leviathan' type. In place of this the old regional cities, many of them very large and widely dispersed, tended to regain their former significance. While the Rhinelands formed the main axis of urban population and industry, the two largest cities were now Hamburg and Munich, in the far north and the far south, respectively (*Figure 2.2*). These two cities, together with Cologne and Frankfurt in the central Rhinelands and one or two others, rapidly emerged as major multifunctional regional capitals.

This spatial dispersal was reflected clearly in the political structure of the new state, emerging under strong supervision by the Western powers. The Federal Republic consists administratively of eleven *Länder*, each of which was given considerable political autonomy. Although dating only from the post-war period, they are based on the historic German states, and their capitals are cities which have long been centres of economic, political and cultural life. Their renewed buoyancy in the context of the Federal Republic has tended to diminish the attractive capacity of the more centrally placed areas and to foster the spread of economic activity more widely throughout the country. There was a deliberate decentralization of the government apparatus and of cultural and educational institutions and the media[4]. The federal capital, Bonn, was dubbed 'the federal village', and with its population of 115 000 it was of little symbolic significance to the state[5]. The constitution of 1949 also gave the Bonn government limited powers with the deliberate intention of discouraging that growth of centralism which had been such a feature of the country's slide towards aggression and war.

Thus the German Federal Republic, which at the time of the Schuman Declaration had been in existence for only one year, was in virtually every way different from France. It was new, planned rather than the product of evolution, and had a decentralized federal structure which fitted in with its historical development. It was urbanized, populous and industrial, rich in resources, particularly energy, and potentially the workshop of Europe. It was largely designed by the victors as a compromise between solving the historic problem of German aggression and enabling the country to make its contribution to the Western Alliance. However, with the uncertainties about the future and the considerable potential power of the new state, France and others had very real doubts at the time as to its effectiveness as a permanent embodiment of the spirit of the 'good little Germanies'.

Italy, the third of EC(6)'s 'big three', had roughly the same area and population as West Germany, but it was chronically weak and under-industrialized compared with its two trans-Alpine neighbours. It was also separated from them, and from the rest of northern Europe, by the Alpine barrier. Until the later nineteenth century Italy had remained, in Metternich's phrase, 'a geographical expression', divided into small states and subject to continual foreign interference. Following the development and eventual triumph of Italian nationalism, expressed heroically in the exploits of Garibaldi, most of the peninsula was in 1860 united into a single state. Rome was not incorporated until ten years later, when the Franco–Prussian war brought about the providential removal of the French garrison protecting the Pope. The attitude of Piedmont, the Kingdom of Sardinia, was crucial throughout the whole process. It was the consolidation and expansion of this Italian version of Prussia, led by its Bismarck, Camillo Cavour, and drawing strength from the romantic nationalism associated with Garibaldi, which was responsible for the creation of the Italian state. The 'Piedmontization' of Italy which followed was to continue after 1870, when the capital was, for reasons of geography and history, moved to Rome.

The new state consisted of two quite distinct parts, the north and the south, separated from one another by a sort of intermediate transition zone. The north, and in particular the upper Po region, was the most economically developed, industrialized and politically mature, and it rapidly became the country's leading region, with Milan as its major business and financial capital. While it lacked the coal and iron base of northern Europe's heavy industrial regions, it did possess certain advantages, including a long urban and commercial tradition, the great port of Genoa and relative proximity to transalpine Europe. There was also the great potential of the Alps for the production of the hydroelectricity which was shortly to be harnessed.

In complete contrast to this there was the Mezzogiorno, Italy south of Rome, together with the islands of Sicily and Sardinia (*Figure 2.3*). Until unification it had been the Kingdom of the Two Sicilies, a backward and foreign-dominated state which had been out of the mainstream of forward developments in Europe throughout the nineteenth century. The area was remote, poor, underdeveloped, in places malarial and overpopulated in terms of its limited economic capacity. It was from this region that the greater part of the massive emigration from Italy to the rest of Europe and the New World took place. Thus, like Germany, Italy, established at almost exactly the same time, consisted of two distinct parts. However, while in Germany each had contributed particular qualities to enhance the strength of the new state, in Italy the strength of the north was in almost all ways so great that it was able to secure overwhelming and lasting dominance over the weak south.

Italy increasingly sought nationalist and imperialist solutions to its problems, and this culminated in the Fascist administration of the inter-war years. However, by the time of World War II the inherent weaknesses still remained, and the bombastic and aggressive foreign policy of Mussolini turned out to have been a distraction rather than a cure. Mussolini's dream of *mare nostrum*[6] turned into a nightmare in which Italy became merely a pawn in the far more sinister German attempt to secure European hegemony. Italy was a backward state masquerading as a great power, and

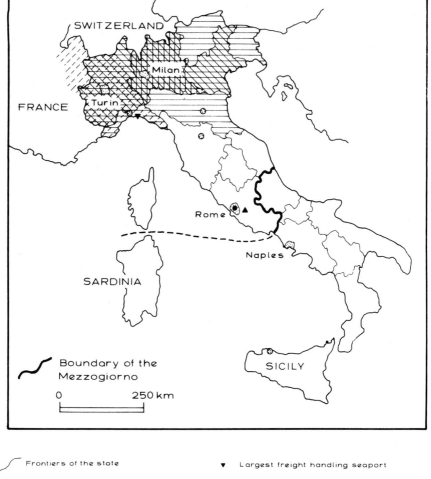

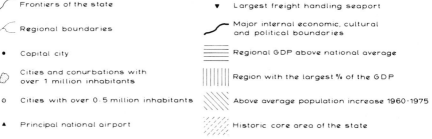

Figure 2.3 The spatial structure of Italy

her total defeat exposed her weakness for all to see. In 1950 over a third of the population still gained a living through agriculture and a smaller proportion was engaged in industry than in any other country of the EC(6). The Italian coal output of 1.2 million tons and steel production of 2.4 million tons were small fractions of those of either West Germany or Britain. Even more serious, the gap between north and south was as great as ever, and this 'two nations' situation remained one of the greatest of the country's social as well as economic evils.

The other three members of the EC(6) were Belgium, the Netherlands and Luxembourg – the Benelux countries. They are on quite a different scale from the Community's 'big three'. Their combined area of 65 000 km^2 is only one-eighth that of France alone. Their much greater significance in human terms was reflected in their total population of 20 millions in 1950, which was half that of France at the time. In order to further their collective interests as small states surrounded by much bigger ones they had in 1948 founded the Benelux Union, which was to become a prototype for future supranational developments. It established a free trade area together with economic, political and other forms of cooperation and policy coordination. The grouping possessed considerable unity deriving from contiguity and geographical location, but the geographical features of each of the members were in many ways very different.

While deriving from the quasi-colonial political entity of the southern Netherlands, Belgium is a relatively young state, dating only from 1830. It and adjacent lands had gained the sobriquet 'cockpit of Europe', and it had come to be a buffer and frequently a battleground for the surrounding great powers. Following an unsuccessful attempt after the Napoleonic Wars to unite it with the Kingdom of the Netherlands to the north it was given sovereignty by the powers and its neutrality guaranteed. It has in reality little unity, either physically or culturally, and is, like Germany, a slice – albeit a very small one in this case – through northern Europe. It consists of two contrasting physical units, the northern lowlands, centring on the composite delta of the Rhine, and the Hercynian mountains of the Ardennes. Culturally this division is paralleled by the distribution of Dutch-speaking Flemings in the north and the French-speaking Walloons in the south (*Figure 2.5*). The actual linguistic divide, however, is north of the physical discontinuities in the present landscape. Relations between the two language groups have never been easy, and were made worse after the establishment of the modern Belgian state by the Francophone dominance. This resulted both from the predominance of French influence at the time and from the development of the southern coalfield in Wallonia to become one of the most advanced industrial areas on the Continent. This uneasy state has been held together shakily by a dynasty of German origin from their centrally placed capital of Brussels, a predominantly French-speaking city located uncomfortably just to the north of the linguistic divide.

The country's central location gave it from the outset considerable significance in the affairs of north-west Europe. Its considerable natural wealth grafted onto its historic, industrial and commercial traditions was rapidly to make it also of considerable economic importance. Despite its small size it had by the end of the nineteenth century become an important industrialized country, and it played an important role in the commercial and imperial activity of the time. Throughout the first half of the present century it remained a major industrial country with a large coal and steel output. By 1950 its coal, steel and iron output were nearly half as great as those of France and, of course, far greater than those of Italy. It had one of the highest proportions of the labour force in industry and one of the lowest in agriculture in the whole of the EC(6), and productivity in agriculture was very high, especially in the fertile north of the country.

The minute state of Luxembourg is about the size of an average English county. It had maintained its independence over the centuries largely because its capital was one of Europe's most impregnable fortresses, and this independence was recognized by the powers in 1867. In order to be economically viable it has had to seek some accommodation with one or other of its neighbours. It was initially within the German customs union, but this arrangement was terminated after World War I. In 1923 a successful arrangement was negotiated with Belgium, and the Belgo–Luxembourg Economic Union (BLEU) came into existence. The large deposits of Jurassic iron ore in the south of its territory has given Luxembourg a greater economic importance than the size of its territory would otherwise indicate. A large iron and steel industry has been built around these deposits and in 1950 the country was producing 6 million tonnes of iron ore and 2½ million tonnes of steel. It thus made an impressive contribution to the output of ECSC as a whole.

The Netherlands is very different physically, historically and economically from the other two Benelux countries. It is an old state created by the Dutch revolt against the Spaniards in the sixteenth century. It is almost entirely within the North European plain and centres on the composite delta of the Rhine. A federal state, originally the 'United Provinces', its economic and political heart was the province of Holland in the west, and this was the main centre of that impressive commercial activity which reached its zenith in the late seventeenth century. The fluvial and deltaic deposits underlying its territory enabled the development of an intensive and specialized agriculture, which also contributed to the country's considerable wealth. In the nineteenth century, lacking as it did the geological requirements for heavy industry, the country came to be economically overshadowed by its southern neighbour, Belgium. This did not prevent the further development of its agriculture for the production and export of specialized products. As a result a relatively large section of its population came to be engaged in agriculture and a relatively smaller one in industry. The small Limburg coalfield made a contribution to the country's energy requirements, but heavy industry was little in evidence. As a consequence of the traditional and continuing importance of commercial activity, especially that associated with the great ports of Rotterdam and Amsterdam, after World War II nearly half of the labour force was in the tertiary sector, a larger proportion than in any other Community country.

This, then, is a geopolitical resumé of the six countries which, of the sixteen countries in the non-Communist part of Europe, chose to begin the process of integration at the beginning of the second half of the present century. The reasons for their decision to do so are inherent in their geopolitical circumstances. In the case of France it was above all her perception of the need to control potential German strength coupled with the sense of her own inadequacy, unaided, to accomplish this. Out of this the new idea, the Monnet idea, was born, but its birth was a difficult one, from the full implications of which France subsequently recoiled on a number of separate occasions. In the emerging German Federal Republic, despite the prospects for full economic recovery, there were also many doubts about the efficacy of the project. Fears were expressed of permanent German subservience and, in respect of the EDC, of becoming France's 'European Foreign Legion'. What eventually carried the day was the country's weakness, economically, politically and, above all, internationally along with the prospect of a return to the community of nations. If for France this process was in some ways a 'cage for the German tiger', for the tiger it was a way back into the zoo, and Chancellor Adenauer, among others, also saw economic possibilities in closer ties with Germany's neighbours. Italy, of course, had virtually no coal and little iron and steel, and hoped that the Community would help to redress this unfavourable situation. This internationalism was also a conscious rejection of the autarchic and imperialist policies which had been engaged in throughout the first half of the century. As Bismarck had said, Italy had such a large appetite and such poor teeth, and this had led inevitably to national humiliation. The left wing in Italian politics now looked for the 'wind from the north' to sweep away the remnants of the old outdated system and the right thought that only by 'crossing the Alps' could Italy hope to become a modern European country[7]. For the Benelux countries, as a result of their uncomfortable centrality and consequent vulnerability in intra-European conflicts, the prospect of uniting Europe could not but be a good one. The achievement of a real and lasting peace was bound to be an overall priority for them and well worth any limited sacrifice of sovereignty which it might entail. There was also the importance of international trade and the trading hinterlands of the great port cities of the extended delta stretching down into the Rhinelands and beyond.

In the quarter of a century following the signature of the Treaties of Rome another four states joined the Community and there were a further four applications for membership. This all sprung from a widespread, but by no means universally accepted, belief that membership was, for a variety of reasons, a desirable attainment. By far the most significant new member was, of course, the United Kingdom.

There had been deep reasons for the country's rejection of membership earlier on. Her deteriorating economic position, changing trade patterns and the progressive disintegration of the Commonwealth were the underlying elements in this complete policy reversal. In 1950 Britain was producing more coal and steel than the ECSC countries combined, and its advanced technology was superior to that found in Continental Europe. During the 1950s it began to lose its economic pre-eminence and in 1972, the year before it joined, it produced only 20 per cent as much steel, 40 per cent as much electricity and 30 per cent as many motor vehicles as EC(6). Total United Kingdom foreign trade as a proportion of that of the EC(6) had also fallen from a half to a quarter. Of especial significance was the fall in the proportion of British trade with the Commonwealth. In the middle of the 1950s this had reached a half of the total while by 1972, the last full

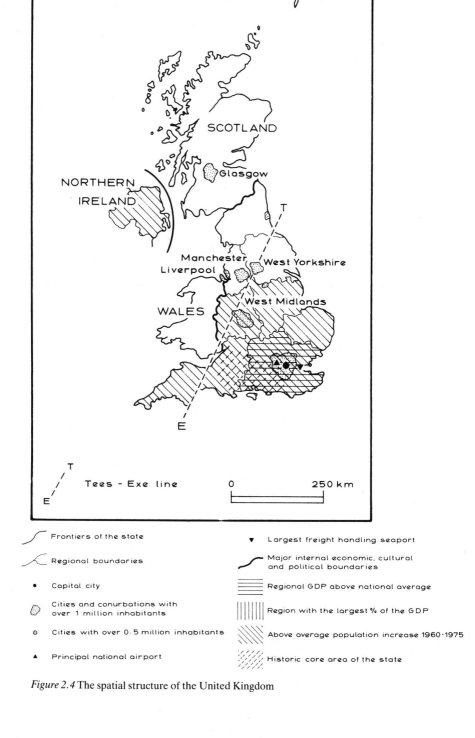

SCOTLAND

Glasgow

NORTHERN
IRELAND

T

Manchester / West Yorkshire
Liverpool

West Midlands

WALES

E

T
/
/
E   Tees - Exe line   0   250 km

⌒ Frontiers of the state	▼ Largest freight handling seaport
⌒ Regional boundaries	⌒ Major internal economic, cultural and political boundaries
• Capital city	☰ Regional GDP above national average
⬠ Cities and conurbations with over 1 million inhabitants	∥∥ Region with the largest % of the GDP
⊙ Cities with over 0·5 million inhabitants	⧄ Above average population increase 1960-1975
▲ Principal national airport	⧄ Historic core area of the state

Figure 2.4 The spatial structure of the United Kingdom

year before membership, it had fallen to 18 per cent. At the same time the proportion of total trade taking place with the EC(6) had been rising from 12 per cent to 21 per cent. In the early 1970s Britain remained fundamentally an industrial country, with 44 per cent of her labour force in this sector, a higher proportion than that of any other Community members except for West Germany and Luxembourg. A major problem was that much of this industry had become uncompetitive, and this was especially true of the older industries such as iron and steel, heavy engineering, shipbuilding and textiles, which had been the foundation of British industrial might in the nineteenth century. These industries were located mainly on or near to the coalfields, and since the 1930s the older industrial regions had been slipping in relation to the more prosperous parts of the country. The Tees–Exe line, the traditional divide between Upland and Lowland Britain, had now come also to be a divide between the more prosperous south-east and the poorer north-west (*Figure 2.4*). Besides the presence of the older industrial areas the problems of this half of the country were compounded by greater overall rural poverty and the fact that Wales and Scotland had vocal nationalist movements which aimed to lessen the economic and political hold of England and especially the south-east. Northern Ireland, the most isolated and atypical part of the United Kingdom, is beset by virtually every regional problem, economic, political, social, cultural and demographic. Since it was set up in 1923 the province has led a troubled and divided existence. In 1969 there was a resumption of that sectarian violence which has increasingly called into question the political viability of this part of the United Kingdom.

The historic national centre in Britain's south-east quadrant had, during the twentieth century, become the principal centre of the island's economic activity (*Figure 2.4*). The 'Coffin'[8], the central axial belt cutting diagonally across the country, linked the industrial areas of the south Pennines via the Midlands with London and the south-east. However, its central and southern parts have shown much greater economic vitality than have those of the north, and this further demonstrates the 'two nations' situation which underlies the problems of contemporary Britain.

The Republic of Ireland entered the Community at the same time as did the United Kingdom. Until 1922 it had itself been a part of this United Kingdom and, following independence, it remained closely dependent on its powerful neighbour. It also remained largely rural and economically and socially backward by the prevailing standards of north-west Europe. The population of 2.8 millions in 1961 was well under half of what it had been in the middle of the previous century before the starvation and emigration resulting from the Potato Famines. While it steadily began to ease itself out of the British orbit, by 1970 over 60 per cent of its external trade was still with its larger neighbour, and Britain's membership of the Communities necessitated that of Ireland also. However, during the 1960s considerable change had begun to take place, and this included the modernization of agriculture, the beginnings of industrialization and the upturn in population which had been declining for well over a century. At the time it became a member the country still remained strongly agricultural with a quarter of the labour force on the land, a far higher proportion by that time than in any other Community country, and contrasting

dramatically with the British 2.7 per cent. The only really large city was Dublin, which had a quarter of the country's total population and in which was concentrated much of the country's industrial and tertiary activity (*Figure 2.5*).

Denmark was the third country to become a member in 1973. This state is both insular and continental, since it consists of the peninsula of Jutland extending out from the North European Plain and a number of islands separating it from Scandinavia. It is an old state, dating back to the tenth century, and it has been traditionally more closely associated with its Scandinavian neighbours to the north than with the adjacent continent. This association has taken political, economic and cultural forms, and it largely explains why the capital city and historic centre of Denmark are located on the island of Sjaelland, and highly peripheral in relation to the territory of the present Danish state. The establishment of the Nordic Council after World War II led to a reinforcement of the relationships among the Scandinavian countries. This situation, coupled with the fact that Britain was the major export market for Danish agricultural produce, made Community membership initially unattractive to the Danes. As was the case with Ireland, the prospect of British membership changed Danish perceptions of the Community, and this was reinforced by the anticipation that Norway, also a member of the Nordic Council, would be joining at the same time. The Norwegian referendum's rejection of membership, the continuing ties with the rest of Scandinavia and the dislike of certain EC policies soon produced disaffection in many quarters with Community membership. The position of Denmark as a link between north and south, between Scandinavia and the Continent has proved to be a difficult one to sustain. It has become the source of many problems as Denmark has evolved from being largely a specialized agricultural country to one in which there is considerable industrial development.

Greece became the tenth member of the Community in 1981. Although it was the country in which European civilization began, it was subsequently under Byzantine and Turkish domination for centuries. The modern Greek state dates only from 1830, and it did not achieve its present frontiers until 1918. By the standards of north-west Europe this is a poor and underdeveloped country. As recently as the middle of the 1960s over a half of the labour force was on the land and under one-fifth in industrial activities. However, there is a strong maritime and commercial tradition, centring especially on Athens/Piraeus in the south and Thessaloniki in the north, and these have been the centres of modern development. By the early 1980s the proportions of the national labour force in agriculture and industry were both about a third of the total. The developments of the years following World War II have been especially associated with the growth of Greater Athens, which now contains about 3 million people, a third of the country's population. Widespread depopulation of the country-side and the islands has taken place in favour of this enormous metropolis, which is now the fifth largest in the whole of the European Community (*Figure 2.5*). It now has a nearly total dominance in virtually all spheres of Greek life, the only other city of significance being Thessaloniki in the far north. For a relatively underdeveloped country like Greece, Community membership, entailing as it does competition from the far stronger economies of north-west Europe, carries many risks. This has been reflected in the divisions of political opinion on its merits, much of the debate having the familiar left/right dichotomy. However, the country had been an associate member of the Community since 1962, and full membership was always considered the ultimate goal. It was judged by the right wing New Democracy[9] party that the Greek economy could be modernized more effectively within the Community than outside it, and that being 'in Europe' also had less tangible, but nonetheless real, advantages for a small and potentially vulnerable state in the eastern Mediterranean. If the Italian remedy in the 1950s had been to 'cross the Alps', then Greece by the same token has in the 1980s to 'cross the Balkans'. Greek membership can also be seen as signifying a wider statement to the effect that Greece, although on the periphery of Europe, as currently defined, and over the centuries subject to oriental influences, wishes itself now to be considered as a European country.

National moods and attitudes are notoriously subject to considerable short-term change, and resulting changes of government in democratic countries frequently result in new policies. In contrast, the mills of geographical change grind slowly, but they grind impervious to the vagaries and swings of political opinion. Since the 1950s changes have been occurring in the spatial structures of the Community's member countries and these have been of much significance as factors underlying attitudes to membership and to the future integration of Europe.

In France the Paris/provinces dichotomy remains, and the Paris region has grown considerably. While the old city itself has decreased in size, the extended Paris region has increased. It now contains some 10 million people, nearly one-fifth of the national total. The radial concentration of the road and rail networks on the capital, for long such a marked feature of the country's transport geography, has now been further reinforced by motorways and air routes. The Seine, downstream of Paris, is the country's most important inland waterway, and Le Havre remains the country's second port after Marseille. It was in order to counteract just this *unicéphalisme*[10] that the French plan for regional development established eight *métropoles d'équilibre* in an attempt to reinvigorate the provinces[11] (*Figure 2.1*). Since the 1960s the populations of these towns and cities have been increasing faster than that of Paris itself, and they have been the principal foci for development in their vicinities. As the old coal- and steel-based industries have contracted so the north-eastern industrial region has declined and become itself something of a problem region. As the major counterweight to the dominance of Paris it has been replaced by the south-east of the country, in particular the Rhône valley south of Lyon together with the delta, parts of the Mediterranean coast and the French Alps. This has led to the concept of *les deux Frances*, divided by a line from the Seine estuary to the Rhône delta[12]. To the east of this the greatest amount of industrial growth has taken place. Here also has taken place the most immigration, the largest population increase, the fastest urbanization and the largest growth in average standards of living. In contrast, to the west of this line, and especially in the Massif Central, Brittany and parts of the south-west, there has been far less change. Agriculture has retained its important position, there has been less industrialization and there has been population loss by emigration to Paris and other large cities in the east. The importance of the Paris–Lyon–Marseille axis has been reinforced with motorway, pipeline and electric and high-speed rail connections. As a coast-to-coast line of communication it has been important in linking together the Seine and lower Rhône industrial areas and in helping to stimulate the impressive development of the south-east of the country.

The great development since World War II is reflected in the demographic resurgence. Between 1950 and 1980 the population increased by one third – from 40 to 54 millions – a faster absolute increase than occurred during the whole of the previous century. The largest proportion of this increase has been to the east of the Seine–Rhône line, and it has been mainly urban. Over this period also the proportion of the labour force engaged in agriculture has declined from a third to under one-tenth.

In 1950 the German Federal Republic was not yet a fully sovereign state, and her economy was only beginning to recover from World War II and the vacillations in Allied policy towards her. Ten years later, for the third time in three-quarters of a century, she had resumed her position of economically the strongest state in Western Europe. The coal, steel and heavy industries upon which this strength had been based until then were now powerfully reinforced by a massive expansion of secondary manufacturing. Passenger cars, commercial vehicles, radios, televisions, cameras and domestic equipment had now become the basis of the West German *Wirtschaftswunder*[13], and the country was responsible for nearly half of the exports of the EC(6) in these sectors. This booming industry centred on the great regional cities and industrial areas of the Rhinelands, notably Cologne, Frankfurt, Stuttgart and Düsseldorf, together with Bremen, Hamburg and Munich. The new developments had come to focus on the north–south Rhine axis, which contrasted markedly in character and orientation with the east–west (Ruhr–Berlin) axis promoted in the conditions of a united Germany[14]. The new state had also developed a marked westerly orientation in the growth of commercial and industrial activity and the movement of population. This latter began with the influx of refugees from the 'lost lands' after 1945 and the subsequent expulsion of 9.6 million Germans from them. This was followed by an emigration to the West from the Soviet zone, which had reached some three millions by 1961 when the Berlin Wall was built to staunch the flow. In large part as a result of these east-to-west movements, the territory covered by the Federal Republic, which in the late 1930s had a population of 43 millions, was, by the 1970s, supporting 62 millions. The old heartlands of Germany around the Iron Curtain had become unattractive both to those driven from the east and as locations for new enterprise. The result was that the belt adjacent to the Iron Curtain has been designated as a development area, the *Zonenrandgebiet*, and is a recipient of regional aid from federal funds (*Figure 2.2*).

Major exceptions to the westerly orientation and the pre-eminence of the north–south axis are the two largest cities in the country, Hamburg and Munich. The continuing growth and prosperity of both of these, one the country's largest seaport and the other a major regional centre, is testimony to the fundamentally devolved character of the state. While Bonn is the federal capital, national functions are actually spread widely, and such cities as Hamburg, Cologne, Frankfurt and Munich are important national centres of governmental and other activity. West Berlin has come to be considered for most purposes as a part of the Federal Republic, and in the Federal constitution it is referred to as 'the capital of Germany'. This assertion is intended to leave open the possibility of a united Germany at some future date. Its status as a capital city has been maintained by the locating there of national cultural institutions, government departments and the headquarters of firms. However, during the 1970s, and particularly following the four-power agreement of 1972[15], the significance of the city began to decrease. The Federal Republic had now developed the spatial structure of a discrete state, with its own internal balance and growing sense of permanence. This, together with the markedly western spatial orientation was making Berlin increasingly out on a limb, even an embarrassing irrelevance to the new generation of rich and prosperous West Germans. This diminished status has been reflected in the decrease in the population from 2.2 millions in 1961 to 2.0 millions in 1980, and, with the birth rate going down, the average age of the population is increasing. This has been happening at a time when the population of West Germany has been increasing rapidly. West Berlin is now only slightly larger than Hamburg (pop. 1.8 million) and Munich (pop. 1.6 million). Until the 1960s West Berlin's principal problems were the political and military ones of the survival of a Western enclave east of the Iron Curtain. Since the 1970s it has had to adjust itself to the position of being an outlier of a Federal Republic which considers itself to be, and has the geopolitical characteristics of, a fully fledged state.

Since the 1950s the economic position of Italy has perhaps changed more fundamentally than has that of any other EC member state. At the end of World War II it remained backward and weak by north-west European standards, but during the quarter of a century following 1950 it entered the ranks of the major industrialized states. This was achieved in large measure through the bringing into use of new technology which was able to go a long way towards rectifying the inherent weaknesses which had for long held her back. In particular there were the further exploitation of the country's indigenous energy resources, such as Alpine hydroelectricity; the construction of coastal heavy industrial complexes, especially for oil refining and steel manufacture, to take advantage of low cost imports of energy and raw materials; and the planning and execution of a comprehensive motorway network. These were the three principal foundations upon which the impressive expansion of manufacturing industry was based. Over this period an attempt has also been made to tackle the problem of that north–south dichotomy which has plagued Italy since it became an independent state. Italian regional policy since the 1950s has focused upon an attempt to develop the south through the agency of the *Cassa per il Mezzogiorno*[16]. There have been massive transfers of funds from both Italian and foreign sources, and the result has been considerable modernization. Motorways have been constructed, railways electrified, agriculture improved and industrial growth stimulated. In spite of the great strides which have been made, the relative positions of north and south have not appreciably changed. The north remains without question the centre of the country's industrial and commercial strength, the location of its principal financial centre and the headquarters of the major companies. It has the highest levels of urbanization, the most developed communications infrastructure and the highest average standards of living (*Figure 2.3*). Since the 1950s the area has also accrued further relative advantage by drawing in resources, particularly labour, from the south, and maximizing the utility of its own indigenous resources, particularly energy. As a result of its location it has more than any other part of Italy been able to 'climb the Alps', and the spectacular improvements in transalpine communications within the context of the European Community have bound it ever closer to northern Europe. This is evidenced in the development of 'euroports' at Genoa and Trieste and the motorways, pipelines and electrified railways now burrowing through the Alps. Thus the desire of the Italian leaders in the early 1950s to seek national salvation by looking to the north has achieved and maintained clear spatial expression in the orientation of the Italian state in the 1980s.

A major change which has taken place in the Benelux countries since the 1950s has been the considerable alteration in the relative positions of Belgium and the Netherlands. Following the establishment of ECSC, Belgium's southern coalfield, the source of the greater part of the country's energy requirement, faced great problems caused by imports of the more efficiently produced German coal. As in the case of the adjacent French Nord coalfield, this had an adverse effect on the old industries of iron and steel, engineering and textiles. In contrast, the north of the country, up to then relatively less prosperous, has enjoyed considerable new growth. This has been especially favourable to the Antwerp–Ghent–Ostend–Bruges quadrilateral, where considerable new industrial growth, much of it related to the advantage of coastal locations, has taken place. As a consequence, the economic centre of the country has now moved from French-speaking Wallonia to Dutch-speaking Flanders. Brussels, on the hinge between the two, has maintained its position as capital, largest city and major commercial and financial centre. Since the 1950s it has, of course, also gained considerably from being in addition an international city, and a large proportion of the wealth generated now comes from this function. In a very similar way Luxembourg has suffered the decline of its heavy industry and its iron ore extraction, but has more than compensated for this by the growth of its new international functions.

While Belgium has suffered from the difficulties posed by the decline of its old heavy industrial base, the Netherlands has not had this kind of albatross on anything like the same scale. While industrialized Belgium had flourished in the early part of the century, the more agricultural Netherlands had been less prosperous. The great transformations of the Industrial Revolution had, to a large extent passed it by. After World War II, however, it was the recipient of the same kind of coastal and riverine growth which has made northern Belgium far more prosperous than the south. The result has been great growth in the cities of the Randstad[17] in south Holland and especially around Rotterdam-Europoort, the largest port complex in the European Community, with its enormous commercial hinterland stretching into the Rhinelands. This is another country which has experienced fast population growth, from 10 millions in the early 1950s to 14 millions in the early 1980s. This 40 per cent increase has brought the population of the Randstad to 5.7 millions, over 40 per cent of the total population of the country, further emphasizing that western orientation which has been a feature since the seventeenth century. The east has remained relatively more lightly populated, less industrialized and more agricultural. The only major industrial growth there has been along the Rhine–Maas axis eastwards to include Arnhem, Nijmegen, Tilburg and Eindhoven.

The main features of the spatial structures of the four newer Community members at the time of their entry have already been considered. It has been seen that profound changes had been occurring in Britain's spatial structure since the 1930s, and these largely continued after the country's membership. The demographic 'drift to the south' had already effectively finished by the mid-1960s, and there is little sign of any reverse trend occurring. As one might have expected, membership of the Community has stimulated that part of the country nearest to the Continent, with which new relationships have been increasingly forged. The south-east quadrant of Britain continues to maintain its pre-eminence in most aspects of national activity together with the lowest average unemployment and the highest standards of living. However, considerable change has been taking place in the resource situation, and especially in the output of indigenous energy. This centres on the British section of the North Sea Energy Basin, which is taken to include not only the submarine resources of oil and natural gas but also the coal along the eastern flanks of England. These enormous resources have now combined to make Britain self-sufficient in energy, producing 157 million tonnes oil equivalent (oe) as compared with 108 million tonnes in 1972. This makes Britain by far the most energy-rich country in the Community, with an indigenous output of four times that of France and seven times that of Italy. This energy situation is not that dissimilar from that of Britain in the 1900s, when the country's coal output was by far the largest in the whole of Europe. However, there has been a considerable alteration in the spatial distribution of the energy resources in each case. While the major coalfields of the coal age were those of northern and western Britain, the principal exploited energy resources are now to be found to the east, from the Shetlands southwards through eastern England to the southern North Sea. The distribution of coal production contributed strongly to the country's western orientation at the time, while the current distribution of exploited energy has contributed, along with other factors, to its replacement by an eastern orientation. Apart from the growth of the indigenous energy industries, Britain's position has continued to slip. By the early 1980s Britain was responsible for some 16 per cent of the GDP of the EC(10) and 6 per cent of its total external trade. This compares with 26 per cent and 29 per cent in 1961, the year of the country's application for membership.

Unlike Britain's generally declining position, in Ireland the process of industrialization and modernization which was set in train in the 1960s has been accelerated since membership. The proportion of the labour force engaged in agriculture has fallen from a quarter to a fifth, and that in industry has edged up. The process has been greatly helped since 1973 by the large transfers of funds from Community agencies and the new market for Irish goods which has opened up in Europe. Accompanying this there has been a rapid growth in population, giving it now one of the youngest age profiles in the EC(10). The west of the country remains the most backward and the eastern orientation, focusing on Dublin, has been added to by a southerly one focusing on Cork.

In the case of the two final member states, Denmark and Greece, few general or spatial changes can be registered since membership. In both countries the capital cities and their regions have an absolute dominance over national affairs, and this they retain despite attempts to stimulate development in Jutland and Macedonia, respectively (*Figure 2.5*). Arhus and Thessaloniki are second cities well outside the zones of influence of the respective capitals and they have been developed as regional growth poles with limited success. There the resemblance between the two countries ends, since Denmark has the highest per capita GDP in the Community and Greece has the lowest. While a principal concern of Denmark is that of identity, of establishing her position in Europe while remaining a member of the Nordic Council, that of Greece is of catching up with the rest of Europe and with using the Community to help her to achieve this.

Notes

1. J.-F. Gravier, *Paris et le Désert Français*, Paris, 1947
2. The effects on French attitudes of the openness of the northern frontier and the consequent vulnerability of Paris is dealt with by Raymond Aron in *Peace and War*, London, 1966
3. 'A sour sandy soil on which brutal manorial chiefs and brutish serfs fought a dour and relentless battle with nature and with each other' (J. A. R. Marriott and C. G. Robertson, *The Evolution of Prussia*, Oxford, 1915). Voltaire had acidly referred to Frederick the Great of Prussia as the 'roi des lisières' (King of the swamps)
4. The high levels of decentralization in the German Federal Republic can be judged from the locations of some of the country's major institutions and activities. While the Federal Capital is in Bonn, the Federal Audit Office and the National Library (the German Library) are located in Frankfurt, which also has the country's leading international airport. The Constitutional and Supreme Courts are in Karlsruhe and the Federal Police Office is in Wiesbaden. Hamburg and Frankfurt are the centres of the national press, all other publishing centres being regional. Berlin has the most important national museums and cultural institutions, but radio and television stations are located in all the *Länder* (see also Chapter 3, note 2)
5. It was, of course, chosen for just this reason. Its main historic claim to fame is that it was the birthplace of Beethoven, and it was this tradition of Germany as a civilized European country which the Western powers had wished to revive after World War II
6. The idea that the Mediterranean was an Italian sea implied the recreation of the Roman Empire in modern form. Fascism had been named after the *fasces*, the bundle of sticks with an axe which was a symbol of authority in ancient Rome
7. F. R. Willis, *Italy Chooses Europe*, New York, 1971
8. A term coined by Professor E. G. R. Taylor to describe the changes which were then taking place. See E. G. R. Taylor, 'Discussion on the Geographic Distribution of Industry', *Geographical Journal*, **93**, 1938
9. New Democracy was established in 1974 after the end of the rule of the Colonels. Led by Constantine Karamanlis, it became the principal right of centre party in the country
10. 'Single-headed' or centrally controlled, as demonstrated by the concentration of the country's cerebral activity in Paris. *See* Chapter 3, note 2
11. The eight *métropoles d'équilibre* were designated in 1964 as part of the fourth National Economic Plan. They are Lyon/St Etienne/Grenoble, Marseille/Aix/Fox, Lille/Roubaix/ Tourcoing, Nancy/Metz/Thionville, Bordeaux, Nantes/St Nazaire, Toulouse and Strasbourg
12. B. and J. L. Kayser, *95 Regions*, Paris, 1971

13. The 'economic miracle' which converted the still weak and devastated Western zones of Germany in the late 1940s into the strong and prosperous German Federal Republic of ten years later. It is particularly associated with the name of Ludwig Erhard (1897–1977). He held the post of Minister of Economic Affairs from 1949 to 1963 and was subsequently Federal Chancellor. He implemented a policy of *Socialmarktwirtschaft* (social market economy)

14. During the 1930s the axis connecting the principal political and industrial centres had been improved, and new industries, such as the famous Volkswagen plant at Wolfsburg, had been developed along it. In 1937 the important Mittelland canal was completed, connecting the Ruhr with Berlin

15. The four-power agreement concluded on Berlin in 1972 terminated the claim that it was still the capital city, and gave it an independent status under the control of the four occupying powers. It was nevertheless agreed that ties between West Berlin and the Federal German Republic should be 'maintained and developed'. For most practical purposes this has meant that West Berlin is treated as a part of the Federal Republic and the regulations of the European Community apply to it in full

16. The *Cassa per il Mezzogiorno* was set up in 1951 for the purpose of tackling the problems of the south of the country. Since then it has remained the principal agency for channelling funds from all sources into the region

17. A huge urbanized area forming a horseshoe from Gorinchem in the south to Utrecht and Zeist in the north. It includes the great cities of Rotterdam, The Hague and Amsterdam

Chapter 3

The component parts: a structural comparison

From the foregoing survey it is possible to observe many similarities in the spatial characteristics of the member states and in the changes which have taken place in them since the establishment of the first Community in 1951. In order to gauge the extent to which there is a pattern behind these similarities, they will first be examined against a theoretical model of the spatial structure of the state.

It is possible to construct a normative model of the spatial structure of the mature isolated state from a synthesis of the ideas of political geographers working in this field (*Figure 3.1*). A fundamental feature of this is the centre–periphery structure identified by Whittlesey[1] and Pounds and developed by analogy from the work of Christaller and von Thünen. This theoretical concept of the state postulates a monadistic unit which has grown exogenously from an annular core region. This germinal core is the heart and motor of the political unit and is likely to be the home of its higher functions[2]. It will probably be the location of the capital city, the largest concentration of population, the most important economic activities, the greatest actual and per capita wealth and the best communications. It will be closely linked with the rest of the ecumene, the major settled and developed part of the state's territory, which contrasts with less settled and developed areas of a 'frontier' character. In the established state population and resources are likely to gravitate towards the core because it is the region of greatest perceived opportunity, while in contrast to this the peripheries will tend to be debilitated by depopulation and an outward flow of resources. Thus, unless other factors mitigate against it, the core is likely to grow in wealth and power at the expense of an ever more impoverished periphery. The development of this situation will be reflected in a radial concentration of the principal internal lines of communication on the core, while inter-peripheral communications usually remain far less comprehensive and effective. Fast modern methods of transport which have been brought into use since World War II, such as motorways, electrified railways and air-routes, may reinforce the locational advantages of centrally placed areas and so further bolster their dominance over the rest of the state's territory. In order to maximize the ease of internal movement the optimum shape for the state is a compact

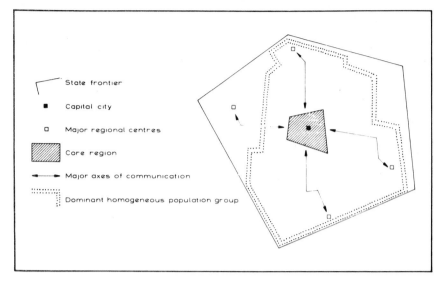

Figure 3.1 Basic model of the spatial structure of the state

one, proximating towards a circle or a hexagon. Within this the core/capital is centrally located so as to facilitate contact with, and control over, the rest of the territory of the state.

In this normative model the greater part of the population of the mature state constitutes a 'nation' which, for our purposes, may be defined as a group having a common language and cultural heritage reinforced in the course of time by shared historical experiences. These characteristics will be inherently different from those of the inhabitants of adjacent states, and such differences, together with associated suspicions and antagonisms, are likely to reinforce the cohesion of the national group. The generic relationship between the nation and the state is a complicated one[3] but the evolution towards a situation of greater internal homogeneity can certainly be regarded as a normative tendency. This partly results from the existence of the state as an independent political unit and partly from the deliberate imposition of uniformity in order to bind its territories together more effectively. Uniform national characteristics are likely to be most developed in and around the generic core or heartland of the state, where the political and economic climate, reinforced by a common history, makes for the highest degree of homogeneity. It is here in the heart of the state that the sacred physical symbols, the iconography of nationhood, are also likely to be most in evidence.

The characteristics so far discussed are all essentially centripetal ones, together reinforcing the monadistic cohesiveness of the state. They will, however, almost certainly be balanced by centrifugal elements tending to have the opposite effect. One of these is the relationship of the periphery to the core. It is likely that within the peripheries there will be less of an automatic identification with the received wisdom of the state and its associated nation. Sub-state national or regional groups may propose alternative identifications and may even identify or relate to similar groups across the frontiers. Peripheral identification with, and loyalty to, the state may also be diminished by the disadvantages perceived to be inherent in the core–periphery dichotomy itself. The idea of the state as represented in the attitudes and values of the core or heartland may come to be regarded as not so much a joint solution to collective problems as, in part at least, a cause of them[4]. The growth of inter-peripheral trans-frontier relationships may exacerbate this situation and fray the state at its edges. Balancing this, centripetally, is the tendency observed for population and other resources to gravitate from the peripheries towards the centre, and so be subjected to cultural absorption by the majority nation. Such a movement will also weaken the relative and actual demographic strength of the periphery and so lessen the effectiveness of peripheral challenges to the core.

Finally, despite such peripheral disaffection, which may make for raggedness at the edges, the mature state actually exists in considerable isolation behind relatively impermeable frontiers. These frontiers, deliberately maintained by the apparatus of the state, will reinforce the other factors, tending to favour internal over external transactions in most areas of contact[5]. This, together with the unifying influences of education and the media, emphasizes the role of the state as the proper sphere for the activities of its people.

Having postulated the model, we will now go on to discuss the extent to which the ten member states of the Community actually conform to it (*Figure 3.2*). In many ways the correlation is a high one, but in others it is clearly far less so. The capital stands out as the largest city in nine of them, the only exception being West Germany's 'federal village'. In six member states the capital is actually over twice as large as the second city (*Table 3.1*). In every one of the member states it is possible to identify a core region which has clear pre-eminence in a wide variety of national political, economic, social and cultural activities. In most cases the core region focuses upon a dominating capital city but in some is rather loosely defined and polycentric. The capital city is located within the core in all the

TABLE 3.1. The incidence of state characteristics in the Community countries

	1	2	3	4	5	6	7	8	9	10
France	x	x	x	x		x	x	x		
West Germany		x	x					x	x	
Netherlands	x		x					x	x	x
Belgium	x		x	x						
Luxembourg	x	x	x	x			x		x	
Italy	x		x	x	x			x	x	x
United Kingdom	x	x	x	x	x	x			x	
Ireland	x	x	x	x	x	x	x	x	x	
Denmark	x	x	x		x	x	x	x	x	x
Greece	x	x	x	x	x	x	x	x	x	x

Key to state characteristics (1 to 10)

1 = Capital largest city in the state	6 = Radial communications network
2 = Capital over twice the size of next largest city	7 = Unitary internal political structure
3 = Identifiable core region	8 = Predominant homogeneous population group
4 = Peripheral characteristics clearly identifiable	9 = Total national homogeneity
5 = Mainly hard frontiers	10 = Absence of frontier cultural overspill

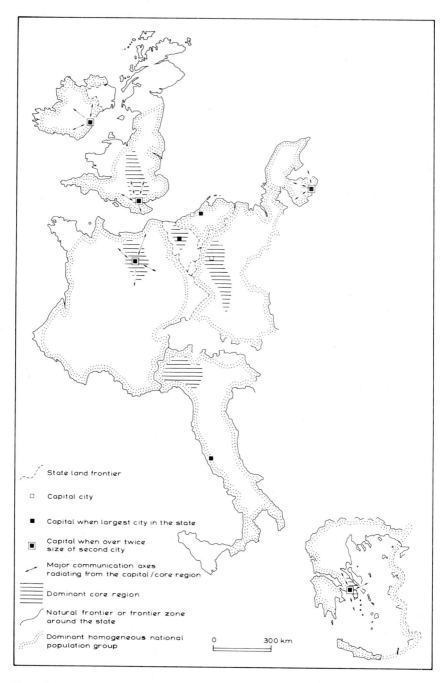

Figure 3.2 The incidence of state characteristics in the Community countries

countries except for Italy and in eight of them the capital/core together have a clear pre-eminence in virtually every important aspect of the national life. The only two exceptions in this are West Germany and Italy. In the former the core is very loosely defined and, as has been seen, a number of important large cities lie outside it. In Italy the capital and the core are geographically remote from one another, and the latter is made up of a number of large industrial and commercial centres. An unmistakably radial communications network centring on the capital/core can also be identified in seven of the countries. In six countries there are large contiguous areas having the peripheral characteristics of population and resource outflow and which display the symptoms of regional debility associated with such a situation.

As to the characteristics of the population, there is almost total national-type homogeneity in seven countries, while one other, France, is fairly close to this. The United Kingdom has four major national-type components and a number of regional ones, and although this makes the homogeneity score low, the anglicization of the whole state territory has, in fact, been nearly total. Only in Belgium is there no tendency whatsoever to national homogeneity. Around only six states do the frontiers constitute largely 'hard' barriers, and in a majority there are linguistic and cultural overlaps into neighbouring countries.

If all ten characteristics of the state model as itemized in *Table 3.1* are considered together, than 67 per cent of them are to be identified clearly in EC(10) as a whole. On average some two-thirds of the selected features are possessed by each member state. However, their actual incidence varies greatly, from 100 per cent in Greece to as little as 30 per cent in Belgium. The characteristics whose incidence are greatest are a core–periphery structure (90 per cent), the pre-eminence of the capital city (80 per cent) and the existence of a homogeneous (national) population group (80 per cent). Characteristics with the lowest incidence are the existence of 'hard' frontiers, a radial communications network and a unitary political structure, each of which has only a 50 per cent incidence.

There are also interesting spatial variations in the incidence of characteristics through the Community. In the original six countries the overall incidence is 53 per cent, while in West Germany and the three Benelux countries it is down to only 46 per cent (*Table 3.1*). In these four countries, therefore, there is on average a greater tendency to deviate from than to conform to the model. Among the countries of EC(6) France stands alone by virtue of its 70 per cent correspondence to the model, and in the 30 per cent which is recorded as negative, the degree of deviation is actually slight.

In contrast to this situation in the original members, the four members which subsequently joined have collectively an 87.5 per cent correspondence. In the three smaller countries the correspondence averages over 90 per cent, while that of the United Kingdom is, significantly, just the same as France.

Thus, as a general statement, correspondence to the normative state model can be seen to be lowest in the oldest and most centrally located member states, while in the newer and more peripheral ones it is on average nearly two-thirds greater. Belgium, the Community's most centrally located state, has only one-third the correspondence of Greece, the most peripheral one. A generalization can be made that enthusiasm for Community membership appeared initially to be in inverse proportion to the presence of the spatial characteristics associated with the mature state. In spite of this, it is significant that the Community's seminal state, France, comes out with a relatively high rating, while its major opponent in the 1950s, the United Kingdom, while scoring less than the other newer members, has about the same rating as France.

While on average two-thirds of the characteristics of the model are then present in the member states, in a number of them the incidence has been seen to be very low indeed. There is also another factor which must be taken into consideration in assessing the relationship of membership to spatial characteristics. This arises from the changes which have been taking place since the early 1950s and their spatial implications. These are the changes which, as was seen in the last chapter, have produced such phenomena as *les deux Frances*, the 'drift to the south', Randstad Holland, the *Zonenrandgebiet*, the revival of Flanders and many others. These new developments do not always fit readily into the assumptions made by the model. They represent new structures and orientations within states as well as new patterns of external relationships.

The annular centre–periphery state model needs often to be considerably stretched to make allowances for these developments, the more so since the traditionally accepted cores have by no means always been the principal recipients of new growth. In any case what had been grouped together and accepted as being core regions have often actually possessed very different features individually. The Rhineland core of West Germany is a loose, elongated and polycentric region, totally different in its spatial structure from the French core tightly clustered around Paris. Although both possess core-type characteristics, that of France reflects the country's long tradition of centralization, with the accompanying *désertification* of the provinces, while, in contrast, the features of the German core accord with and in many ways spring from the essentially decentralized character of the West German state. It forms an axial belt, a chain of conurbations stretched out along the Rhine like a string of beads. Britain's coffin-shaped axis from the south Pennines to London is a similar phenomenon identified as far back as the 1930s. In France the Paris–Lyon–Marseille (PLM) line, now extended northwards to Le Havre, has emerged as the country's principal communications axis, along which are located the largest cities, ports and industrial areas. In Italy also there has been a gradual improvement of communications between the capital city and its northern economic core, and important developments have been taking place along and near to it.

These developments all point to major modifications in the spatial structures of member states. The pre-eminence of central places is showing signs of being replaced by that of important lines of communication, axial belts, linking together the country's most important urban and industrial centres. This in turn points to the desirability of introducing some modifications in the model to accommodate in particular the emerging linear cores (*Figure 3.3*). They appear to have developed as a response to an increasingly undesirable situation within the annular capital/core regions, whose increased size and importance was in part a result of the greater centralization which had been a feature of most European states since World War II. Undesirable manifestations of this include increasing pressures on land use, high infrastructural and social costs and the exacerbation of communication difficulties. There has been a marked tendency since the 1950s for an outward movement of activities from the major cities into their surrounding regions. This has frequently tended to resolve itself into a major thrust of 'core colonization' along a single or composite communication axis. A clear reason for this is the maximization

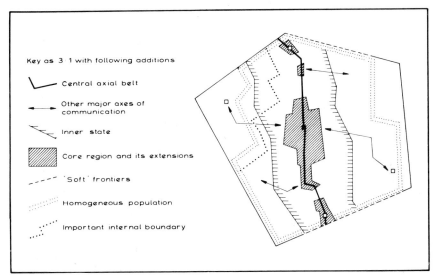

Key as 3 1 with following additions

⟍⟋— Central axial belt

•——▸ Other major axes of communication

⟨ Inner state

▨ Core region and its extensions

- - - 'Soft' frontiers

········ Homogeneous population

········ Important internal boundary

Figure 3.3 Modified model of the spatial structure of the state

of the use of multiple and connected lines of communication available along such an axis, thus decreasing overall infrastructural costs as compared with those of radial networks in which individual lines are likely to be much less used. The emergence of such an axis relates also to the improvement of secondary communications with other parts of the country, and also the appearance of new internal and external orientations. It may both reflect and promote economic growth in regions remote from the core which in contemporary conditions are favoured by location, resources or environment. The axis and the whole area which it influences may appropriately be considered as being an 'inner state' which is an extended and widened linear core region, while the surrounding 'outer state' retains many typically peripheral characteristics.

If one now introduces the concept of the axis into the model then a feature of this sort can be identified in five out of the ten member states (*Table 3.2*). In every one of them the axis contains the capital/core region, the most important ports and exit points and the forward growth areas. In three of them it also contains the country's other largest cities and conurbations. While West Germany is one of the most striking examples of this axial growth, nevertheless the country's two largest cities, Hamburg

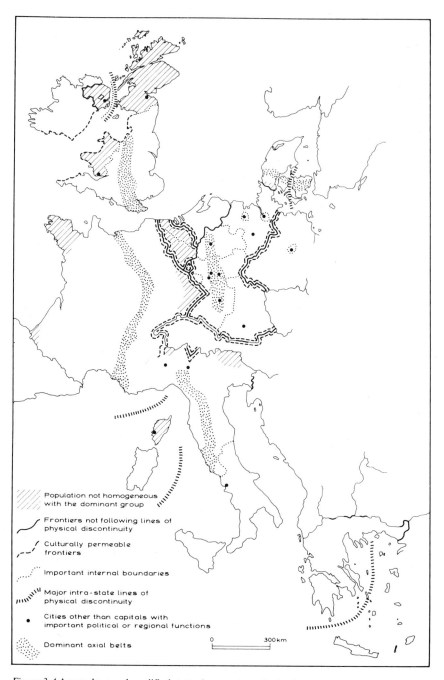

Population not homogeneous
with the dominant group

Frontiers not following lines of
physical discontinuity

Culturally permeable
frontiers

Important internal boundaries

Major intra-state lines of
physical discontinuity

Cities other than capitals with
important political or regional functions

Dominant axial belts

0   300km

Figure 3.4 Anomalous and modified state characteristics in the Community countries

TABLE 3.2. Anomalous and modified state characteristics in the Community countries

	11	12	13	14	15	16	17
France	x	x	x	x		x	x
West Germany		x	x	x			
Netherlands	x		x	x		x	
Belgium			x	x	x	x	
Luxembourg							
Italy		x	x	x	x	x	x
United Kingdom	x	x	x	x	x		x
Ireland				x			
Denmark	x	x		x		x	
Greece				x		x	

Key to state characteristics (11 to 17)
11 = Share of the total population in the capital city tending to decrease
12 = Identification of major axial belt
13 = Identification of growth areas located away from the core region
14 = Established policies for the redress of centre–periphery imbalance
15 = Significant development of regional politico–economic structures
16 = Growth of coastal industrial/commercial complexes to serve the core and axial belt
17 = Presence of the largest cities and conurbations on or near to the major axial belt

and Munich, are located independently of it. In Belgium there is no really predominant axis at all, but a dense multifunctional communications network connecting many nodes. The same can also be seen in the Netherlands, where the network is at its most dense in and around the Randstad (*Figure 3.4*).

The two other countries in which little axial development is easily discernible are Ireland and Greece, and in both the classic core–periphery structure is strongly developed. This situation has tended to become more pronounced in both since the early 1950s, and the predominant position of the capital cities has been reinforced. Significantly, they are both also the poorest, least developed and most geographically peripheral countries in the Community.

In summary it can be said that everywhere the spatial structures of the member states have been in course of change since the 1950s, and this has been most in evidence in France, Italy and the United Kingdom. The changes have been relatively less in the case of West Germany only because of that country's more atypical situation in the first place. The changes focus on the emergence of central axial belts in the more economically developed states. The Benelux countries, and in particular Belgium, are exceptions to this, but this accords with their relatively underdeveloped state characteristics. Considerable development has been taking place along these axial belts and their associated 'inner state' areas have been the recipients of the most economic growth and new wealth generated. They represent a tendency to the resolution of the radial network into one multifunctional line of communications.

The linkage of axial belts and their dendritic extensions to those of other member states represent one aspect of the more general development of transnational contacts within the Community. Its relationship to the emergence of transnational morphological structures and patterns will now be examined.

Notes

1. Whittlesey uses the term 'core region' to indicate the area around which the state had grown. He also refers to the major developed and populous area as the 'ecumene' of the state. See D. Whittlesey, *The Earth and the State*, New York, 1939. The 'central place theory' of Christaller and the 'isolated state' of von Thünen were both attempts to theorize on human spatial behaviour, and the behaviour of the state, although far more complex, is an aspect of this

2. The central institutions of government, Church, education and culture. Paris, for example, is the home of the French head of state, the legislature, the executive and Supreme Court. It has the *grandes écoles* which train the country's administrative and scientific elite, and it is the undoubted centre of the national cultural life. It is not the centre of the Catholic Church in France, since, although Paris is the seat of an archdiocese, the title of premier archbishop by tradition goes to Rheims

3. Traditionally the nation is supposed to have come first and the state to represent the expression of its will to independent existence. However, on occasion the state has itself endeavoured to create a nation in order to justify itself and gain popular support. In many areas there was little sense of being Italian in Italy in the 1860s, and the government had to embark on a programme of 'Italianization'. Mussolini was of the opinion that 'a nation is created by the state which gives real life to a people conscious of its own natural unity'

4. *The Cheviot, the Stag and the Black, Black Oil* (directed by John McGrath, BBC, 1974) puts life into the whole core–periphery predicament in Britain. It deals with peripheral (Highland) bitterness over the centuries towards a hard and domineering establishment which exploits its resources in favour of a remote and alien core region in the south

5. The levels of transactions of all sorts determining the effective regions of human activity. The natural frontiers will be the lines of marked discontinuity in transactions. See K. W. Deutsch, 'Communication and the Concept of a People' (Chapter 11 in W. A. D. Jackson, *Politics and Geographic Relationships*, Prentice-Hall, 1964)

Chapter 4

The geopolitical foundations of unity

The process of European unification, initiated by the Schuman Declaration of May 1950, represented a dramatic *volte face* in the foreign policies of six out of the sixteen countries of the maritime European crescent. It was brought about by the need to resolve certain pressing issues which arose in the years following World War II. It was imperative to reconcile the intra-European conflicts of the first half of the twentieth century with the diminished role of Europe in the emerging bi-polar world order. The process was considerably facilitated by certain elements in the geography of western Europe which were to prove highly conducive to the success of the moves towards unity. Underlying the perception of new geographical realities was the changed European geopolitical situation in the aftermath of World War II.

In the first half of the twentieth century there were in Europe three principal geopolitical macroregions, corresponding roughly to the west, the centre and the east of the continent. The west consisted of the Atlantic frontage, extending over 35 degrees of latitude from northern Scandinavia to southern Iberia. Since the sixteenth century the life of most of this area had been highly orientated towards the Atlantic and the maritime world generally, and much of its political and economic vigour was derived from this maritime association. However, far from being in any sense a political unit, it had come to be divided into ten or so sovereign states each of which handled its affairs largely independently of the others. The region's history had been characterized by considerable inter-state rivalry, and by the beginning of the twentieth century this related in particular to the extra-European roles which the most powerful states had assumed. In addition to this there were also the beginnings of inter-state understandings and alliances, the most significant having been the Anglo–French *entente cordiale* of 1904.

In no small part such understandings were attributable to a fear of the growing power of the central macroregion – *Mitteleuropa*[1]. Historically this had consisted mostly of small or medium-sized states, but since the unification of Germany in 1871 the new German Empire had increasingly come to be recognized as being potentially a destabilizing element in the European balance which had existed since the Congress of Vienna. By the beginning of the twentieth century the power of *Mitteleuropa* had found expression in the Dual Alliance of the German and the Austro–Hungarian Empires, while by the time of World War II it was expressed in the Third Reich, united with Austria by the *anschluss* of 1938 and forming the 'axis' with Fascist Italy.[2]

The hegemonial power of the third macroregion had, since the eighteenth century, been Russia, and her western frontiers had tended to oscillate in accordance with her relative strength in relation to *Mitteleuropa*. After 1918 the Western powers established a shatter belt of new states between the Soviet Union and *Mitteleuropa*, consisting of what Goebbels dismissed as *kleinstaatengerumpel*[3]. The international security of these states had been extremely tenuously maintained, but for the most part they had sought salvation from their predatory neighbours in some form of alliance with the Western powers[4].

During World War II, *Mitteleuropa*, led by Germany, secured a brief ascendancy and, except for the extreme maritime and continental peripheries, for nearly five years controlled the other two European macroregions. The force which it could deploy was, however, insufficient to entrench this domination and the two peripheries, the maritime one aided by the United States, were eventually able to coordinate sufficient resources to bring about the defeat of the centre. The imperial *Mitteleuropa* of 1941 shrank into *Festung Europa* – Fortress Europe – in 1944 and completely disappeared in 1945[5]. The salient geopolitical change resulting from World War II was the total eclipse of *Mitteleuropa* as a force in European affairs. The three Europes became two, separated by the Iron Curtain, and west and east gravitated into the centre to fill the power vacuum created there.

Of the three geopolitical macroregions, the western one had been historically least identified with moves towards a wider continental unity. As has been observed, it had long been divided into distinct and often mutually hostile territorial units, and it was here that the modern European nation state had its earliest development. The territorial states had almost all at some stage become the centres of maritime empires, and this had both made them outward-looking and at the same time magnified their mutual mistrusts. After 1945 the basis of this Eurocentric world system had been undermined by the consolidation of the new world order with its twin centres located in Europe's extended peripheries – America and the Soviet Union. The beginnings of Western European unification, which was a response to this situation, were at first handicapped by the unsolved issue of Germany and in particular by the long-term imbalance between its potential strengh and that of France.

As has been seen, this imbalance derived from factors inherent in the geographies of the two countries, and in particular from the unequal distribution of physical resources. Since the middle of the nineteenth century the most important bases of industrial power had been coal and iron ore, and it was the possession and exploitation of these which largely came to determine the relative strengths of the West European states. Thus Britain became stronger than the Continent, Belgium stronger than the Netherlands and, by the end of the century, Germany stronger than France. Linked to this was the considerable increase in the demographic strength of the industrialized states in relation to the less industrialized; by 1900 the population of Germany was a half as much again as that of France.

On the Continent, the greater part of the heavy industrial resources were highly concentrated into a triangular area stretching from eastern France through the south of Benelux and into western Germany. This Heavy Industrial Triangle was responsible for the overwhelming proportion of the coal, iron ore and steel output of the five countries in the territories of which it was located. By the time of World War II it still accounted for 95 per cent of their iron ore, 85 per cent of their coal and 80 per cent of their steel. Although so valuable to them, this enormous power-house at the same time suffered a number of disadvantages. One of them was that it straddled their frontiers and was consequently highly vulnerable in time of war. Another was that the resources were unevely distributed within it and, on balance, far more favourable to Germany than they were to France and the others. Before World War II the Ruhr coalfield alone had an output of over 100 million tons, far greater than that of the whole of the rest of the Triangle at the time. The German steel output was 26 million tons, which was over twice as much as the other Triangle countries combined and three times that of France alone. Germany also had the natural advantage of a cheap and effective system of water transport centring on the Rhine and its tributaries, while French transport was handicapped by the considerable physical difficulties of communication between the eastern industrial areas and the northern coasts.

During the early part of the twentieth century France had attempted in various ways to rectify the unfavourable situation in which she found herself. In 1918 eastern Lorraine, annexed by Germany in 1871 after the Franco–Prussian War, was rejoined to France and with it came the massive deposits of Jurassic iron ore which had helped build Germany's industrial power in the late nineteenth century. As a result, French iron ore output, which had up to then been quite inadequate, grew within a few years to be twice that of Germany, and her capacity for steel production was correspondingly enhanced. She also assumed economic control of the Saarland with its large coalfield, and in 1923 even occupied the Ruhr itself on the pretext of non-payment of reparations. All this did not, however, prevent the rebuilding of German industrial strength which was, by 1939, to make her yet again the strongest power in Europe. After World War II France once more began to adopt similar policies and, besides the occupation of the zone of Germany allocated to her at Yalta, she again secured economic control of the Saarland and also attempted to gain some permanent control over the Ruhr. Since similar measures had failed to hold down Germany after 1918, the more farsighted French leaders saw that they were scarcely more likely to succeed a quarter of a century later. Rather they saw them as leading once more down the same *cul de sac* towards confrontation, since France clearly still did not possess the physical strength to be able to secure the pre-eminence which she manifestly cherished. It was thus vital that possible alternative solutions be explored with some urgency.

In addition to the concentration of physical resources in close proximity to the frontiers there was also the nature of these frontiers themselves (*Figure 4.1*). These extend in a zone over 650 km in length from the Alps to

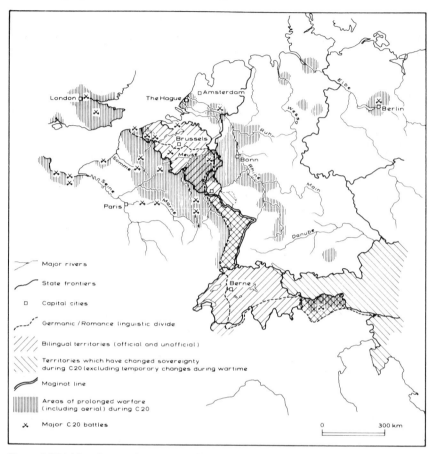

Figure 4.1 Divisive elements in west-central Europe

the North Sea. It widens in the north and south to contain Benelux and Switzerland, but in the centre, over a distance of some 350 km, France and Germany are contiguous. Proximity is important in determining the levels of international interaction, and might have been expected to give rise in the natural course of things to considerable contacts of all sorts. This had, indeed, been the historic situation in this area, but it had been deliberately discouraged by the pursuance of nationalistic policies. The result was an increasing impermeability of the frontiers during the first half of the twentieth century. Yet the frontiers of the zone, separating as they do six independent states, rarely correspond to any underlying physical or human realities on the ground. The French provinces of Alsace and eastern Lorraine are German-speaking, as also is northern Switzerland and the Eupen and Malmédy districts of eastern Belgium (*Figure 4.1*). Letze-burgesch, the old language of Luxembourg, is a Germanic dialect, although French has been the country's official language since 1923. The Walloon population of southern Belgium speaks French, while the Flem-ings of the north speak Dutch, so that neither the Franco–Belgian nor the

Dutch–Belgian frontiers are linguistic or cultural divides. In no case does the frontier zone follow a major physical barrier, and only in one – the river Rhine from Basle to Lauterbach – does it follow a large river for any length. In only one place does it correspond to any underlying reality, and this is the Dutch–German frontier, where it is a linguistic divide.

This central frontier zone does not, then, indicate the existence of genuine territorial divisions in this part of Europe, but represents rather a series of truce lines in the age-old struggle for influence and control over the area. The frontiers were almost entirely subsequent to the settlement and the establishment of the basic cultural character of the zone, and their influence in producing consequent modifications has been a limited one. As a result of their longevity, although inherently weak as lines of discontinuity in human affairs, they have become powerful boundaries in the minds of men. Their territorial unreality is reflected in part in the low scores of the Benelux countries and of West Germany against the spatial model of the state (Chapter 3). The large number of anomalies also suggests a naturally weak insulation against mutual contacts in the area. The regions around these frontiers are far from having the characteristics of peripheries in the spatial model, and their peripherality has been artificially and often laboriously created. On the contrary, they have remained central to the concerns of the adjacent states, and this is confirmed by the persistence of conflict in the area. Their plenitude made them lands of promise, if not promised lands, and their acquisition had remained an age-old ambition.

An examination of the whole of the territory covered by the frontier zone reveals certain deeper transnational geographical realities beneath the dazzle of le Lannou's *états polychromes*[6]. The framework for this is the Rhinelands, the underlying geographical and historical unit shattered by the frontier zone. The river itself flows from the Alps to the North Sea through the Hercynian mountains and the North European Plain (*Figure 4.2*). Together with its tributaries and composite delta it forms a huge hydrographic basin with a total area of $230\,000\,km^2$, about the size of Britain. Together with its main tributary rivers, such as the Mosel, Main and Neckar, it has since early times been a major multipurpose routeway across north-west Europe. As such it has been the vehicle for uniting rather than dividing the riparian lands, and has come to be the centre and axis of a human region in the widest sense[7]. By the beginning of the eighteenth century it possessed a large measure of cultural unity transcending the state frontiers, which had already come to resemble those of the present day. It was predominantly Germanic in speech, but Latin in culture. After the Reformation it had remained mainly Catholic in religion, although Protestant around its Alpine and maritime fringes. Except for France in the west, it was characterized by states which, by European standards, were small or even minute. It was highly urbanized and had a tradition of established city government and free institutions. All in all, it was one of the more prosperous parts of Europe, and was very rich and developed in comparison with the lands immediately adjacent to it. This prosperity was firmly founded on the wealth of its agriculture and industry, but it was also closely linked to the maritime commerce of the delta cities in Flanders and Holland and the transalpine commerce of northern Italy.

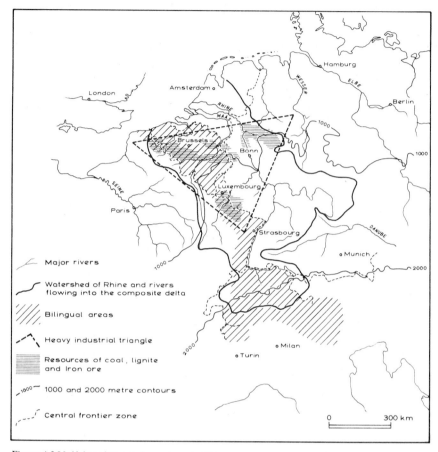

Figure 4.2 Unifying elements in west-central Europe

While politically so divided in modern times, the northern half of the Rhineland had been in the ninth century the heartland of Charlemagne's Frankish empire. Following the Treaty of Verdun in 843 the central Rhineland, together with the adjacent Alps and northern Italy, became the Middle Kingdom, the land of Charlemagne's great-grandson Lothair, who significantly at the same time retained the Imperial crown. This evanescent state of Lotharingia was, however, rapidly eroded by pressures from both west and east, and it soon ceased to exist as a third force in Christendom. In subsequent centuries it was to become the 'cockpit of Europe', a disputed marchland, for the possession of which wars were constantly fought. Today the political fragments of its tenuous independent existence are the three countries of Benelux, forming a buffer zone around the composite delta, and multilingual Switzerland guarding its six hundred years of independence in the mountain fastnesses to the south.

The eclipse of *Mitteleuropa* after World War II, together with the movement of Europe's major geopolitical fault line 300 km eastwards from the Rhine basin to that of the Elbe, revealed more clearly the nature of the former and its relationship to the riparian states. Its physical, commercial and cultural unity was reinforced during the present century by 'industrial Lotharingia'[8] with its valuable resource base (*Figure 4.2*). This has been the essential geographical keystone in the building of European unity. The ideas of Monnet and Schuman implied not merely a coming together of independent territorial states but the giving of a political dimension to the transnational physical and cultural unit which lay beneath their most central areas. This had long been obscured geographically by the polychromatic political dazzle of the states.

In the past the perception of at least some of these realities, and in particular of the power which the possession of such rich resources would confer, had led to attempts by one or other of the riparian states to achieve ascendancy by force. The Hapsburgs, France, the German Empire and the Third Reich all established for a time a measure of control, but were not able to make this permanent[9]. During the present century, attempts to overcome the implications of the geographical reality of Lotharingia and the mutual dependence so strongly implied in its central location and considerable resources are to be seen in the policies of both France and Germany. In order to lessen their dependence on the ports of the Rhine delta the Germans promoted the development of their own North Sea ports. In 1898 they began the construction of the new port of Emden near the Dutch frontier and this was connected to the Ruhr by the Dortmund–Ems canal completed in 1908. At the same time, industrial growth was encouraged in the heartland of the country, in particular around the Saxony coalfield, well away from the western frontiers. Between the wars the *Osthilf* policy was designed to arrest the decline of rural Prussia and to stimulate development in the more backward east of the country. For their part, the French improved the difficult rail link from Dunkirk to Lorraine along the Franco–Belgian frontier to connect the eastern heavy industrial region over French soil with the Nord coalfield and the sea. The output of the small and inefficient coalfields of the Massif Central was also stimulated so as to diminish dependence on the country's only really large coalfield – the Nord – located so uncomfortably close to the vulnerable eastern frontier – the *pont des invasions*[10]. Industrial growth in such apparently safe places as Clermont-Ferrand was encouraged for similar reasons.

'After 1945, ~~however~~, came the belated recognition that war as an attempt to solve Europe's problems could no longer be acceptable in the age of mass terror! Neither attempts to secure control nor avoidance of the implications of physical realities were likely to produce a lasting settlement of the frontier issues and the allied question of resources.'The solution to this was produced, ~~as has been seen~~, by the work of Monnet and his team, and was made acceptable to the various national leaders by the changed geopolitical context in Western Europe. This derived both from the passing of *Mitteleuropa* with its historic drive to achieve power and *lebensraum* in the east and from the running down of the maritime imperial drives of the states of the western frontage. The slice of *Mitteleuropa* west of the Iron Curtain, and more specifically the truncated Federal Republic which was in course of replacing the united Germany after 1949, was a far more acceptable and manageable bedfellow for Western Europe generally and for France in particular. This allowed Europe to be seen, for the first time in centuries, not negatively as territory to be secured and frontiers to be fortified, but positively as the foundation on which to build a structure to replace the former extraterritorial involvements both continental and maritime. As Lukacs put it, Europe was now 'turning inwards . . . confronting herself'[11]. The realization that the European war game was not worth the candle was reluctantly arrived at by the leaders of peoples who had been forced to march to war twice within a quarter of a century, decimating two generations in the process.

The Schuman Declaration predicted that the replacement of conflict by cooperation would 'change the destiny of those regions which for so long have been used for the making of the weapons of war of which they have been most frequently the victims'. Schuman could well speak with feeling, since he was himself a Rhinelander. Born in Luxembourg and reared in Alsace, he regarded himself as 'a representative of the invasion frontier', and in 1950 he was addressing himself above all to another Rhinelander – the West German Chancellor, Konrad Adenauer. Adenauer had since World War I been deeply involved in the region's politics, and had long favoured confederal ideas as opposed to the centralist policies of the Reich. The Italian prime minister of the time, Alcide de Gasperi, was born a citizen of the old Austrian Empire in German-speaking Trentino and educated in Vienna. Other such powerful advocates of unity as Johann Beyen of the Netherlands, Paul Spaak of Belgium and Joseph Bech of Luxembourg were also aware from long and bitter personal experience of the dangers which the 'invasion frontiers' held for their own small countries.

Looked at from the geopolitical viewpoint, the Community idea, the lineage of which stretched from Monnet's original proposals, through the Treaty of Paris and the Spaak Report to the Treaties of Rome, represented an attempt to achieve peacefully from the centre what peripherally-based power had been unable through the centuries to achieve by force. The central thrust towards unity came initially from the Rhinelands, the latter-day Lotharingia. It came from Belgium, the Netherlands and Luxembourg, which had jointly anticipated the Community with their own economic union in 1948; from the German Rhinelands, the core of the emerging Federal Republic, which until the nineteenth century had consisted largely of small independent states deeply suspicious of Prussia's expansionist policies; from Alsace and Lorraine, which had changed nationality four times in seventy-five years as the Franco–German frontier oscillated, and from northern Italy, seminal region of Europe's Renaissance, still permeated by European sentiment and, since 1945, intent on 'climbing the Alps'. In these central lands the feeling of national identity in the old sense was at its weakest, and from them had come some of the most influential exponents of the ideal for a united Europe. Through the unity which Schuman's 'bold act' now began to achieve, these lands started to come into their own in a way they had not really done since Charlemagne's capital was at Aachen, over a thousand years earlier. In the changed context place-names which had been synonymous with conflict – Strasbourg, Luxembourg, Lorraine, the Saar, Eupen and Malmédy – began to acquire a new meaning and a new peaceful significance.

While the epicentre of the Community of Six which emerged in the 1950s was clearly in the northern Rhinelands, the whole central cluster of five countries forms a fairly compact quadrilateral, bounded by the Atlantic Ocean, the North Sea, the Alps and the Iron Curtain[12]. It is nearly coterminous with the continental section of the Northern Sea Lowland, the Community's central physical macroregion (see Chapter 5), General de Gaulle at one stage saw the EC(6) as essentially an alliance of the countries located around the Rhine and the Alps[13], and he appeared to regard the Straits of Dover as an insuperable barrier to its extension. The five countries of this quadrilateral, grouped as they are around the extended hydrographic basin of the Rhine and its tributaries and bounded by mountains to the south and seas to the north, have been naturally involved closely with one another throughout the centuries. Unfortunately, during the first half of the present century this involvement was expressed more in war than in peace. With one exception they had been engaged in both world wars, and all were defeated and subsequently occupied either during or after the second. In the late 1940s they all became, or continued to be, industrial democracies with mixed economies, and all joined the major Western international organizations (see Chapter 1).

The quadrilateral is clearly the hub of maritime Europe, both in physical and in human terms, and from it extend four insular and peninsular arms. The two southernmost of these – Italy and Iberia – are physically continuous with the quadrilateral, while the two northerly ones – the British Isles and Scandinavia – are discontinuous, except only for the peninsula of Jutland. The fact of contiguity has not itself been a controlling factor in Community membership, since the countries of one of the peninsular extensions – Italy – and one of the insular ones – the British Isles – have become members. Italy was, of course, the only one of the four extensions to be a founder-member of the Community and, although peninsular, is nevertheless separated from the countries of the quadrilateral by Europe's highest mountain range. The causes of Italian enthusiasm for Europe following World War II have already been examined, and relate to the economic and political failures of the nationalistic autarchy which characterized the Mussolini regime. Geopolitically it has been facilitated and reinforced by the fact that the country's economic core area is so far north and has a long tradition of close contacts with transalpine Europe. The appeal to this region of 'climbing the Alps' has been made all the greater in recent times by the development and exploitation of the transport technology by which it could be accomplished. Turin and Milan are geographically closer to Lyon and Munich, respectively, than either is to Rome, and the journey times to the northern cities by autostrada are now actually shorter than those to the capital.

The other three extensions were, in the 1950s, far less involved in the matters which preoccupied the countries of the quadrilateral and they consequently did not see much advantage in being bound institutionally to it. However, during the 1960s the stance of the north-western insular extension changed, and in 1973 the two countries of the British Isles attained membership of the Community. This volte face in British foreign policy was as great in many ways as had been that of the 'inner six' a quarter of a century earlier. It was brought about by the delayed perception of the approaching end of the global maritime phase of British history, which had lasted for a quarter of a millennium. In place of this came the perception, at first tentative and indecisive, that the country's future lay with Europe. This was accompanied by internal spatial changes which were effecting the reorientation of the country from the maritime and industrial north-west to the continental and commercial south-east. The Republic of Ireland, of course, joined the Community at the same time as the United Kingdom. This reflected the fact that, even after fifty years of political independence, she still remained in many ways closely bound up with the former imperial power. As it turned out, membership was soon to begin to diminish the scale of that involvement and to open Ireland to wider European contacts.

The north-eastern and south-western extensions from the quadrilateral have remained less involved in the developments centring on it. The membership of Denmark in 1973 was internally controversial and has remained divisive, while the Norwegian referendum of 1972 had rejected the membership which had already been successfully negotiated. As has been observed, Denmark remains a link between the countries of the Nordic Council and those of the Community or, expressed in geographical terms, between Scandinavia and the quadrilateral. The entry of Greece in 1981 thrust the Community deep into the eastern Mediterranean, a region in which the European countries have the roots of their civilization, but with which they have developed only limited contemporary relationships. This has slightly lessened the north-west European dominance in the Community and correspondingly slightly increased the weight of its weaker south.

To Otto von Bismarck, the archetypal nineteenth-century leader steeped in the *realpolitik* of his day, 'Europe' was nothing but a 'fiction', a *notion géographique*. What made the fiction begin to take on reality half a century after the Iron Chancellor's death was the geopolitical fusion of the heart of Europe's western macroregion with the slice of *Mitteleuropa* which found itself on the same side of the Iron Curtain. Thus Monnet's idea for achieving a functional basis for a united Europe, although designed to break the specific deadlock over Germany, was actually firmly embedded in newly emerging political realities. It was by conforming to these underlying realities that the 'bold act' was initially such a surprising success, and what at the time appeared to many hesitant political leaders to be a risky leap in the dark was actually built on far firmer foundations than most of them were at the time aware. The chain of events set in motion by the initial idea was to lead to the release of new collective energies and so to change the international context in Europe. Developments which began and took root in the quadrilateral were subsequently to prove attractive to those states seemingly remote from the geographical and historical circumstances which had given birth to the original idea. This was itself related to the strength of the emerging spatial unity which was generated by the Community and built on its original foundations.

Notes

1. The term used by German geographers to denote not just 'middle Europe' in the physical sense but the wider cultural region dominated by the Germans. It has been variously defined, depending on the exact criteria used, and sometimes it has been taken to include large areas of what is now considered to be Eastern Europe. This was also associated with the search for more *lebensraum* (living space), believed by many at the time to be essential for a densely populated and rapidly developing country like Germany. See R. E. Dickinson, *The German Lebensraum*, Penguin Special, 1943, Chapter 2: 'Mitteleuropa v. Deutschland as the German Lebensraum'
2. The Rome–Berlin axis was the name given to the alliance of Fascist Italy and Nazi Germany. A formal treaty, the 'Pact of Steel', was signed between the two countries in 1939, and this was the basis of their close collaboration throughout World War II
3. 'A rubbish of small states.' They were, in particular, Poland, Czechoslovakia, Hungary, Yugoslavia, Romania and Bulgaria. The first four of these had been established as part of the peace settlement after World War I. Their main crime in the eyes of the Nazis was that they were in the way of German ambitions to achieve *lebensraum* in the east
4. *See* Chapter 1, note 6
5. Mussolini had been overthrown in 1943, and the new Italian government surrendered to the Anglo–Americans who had by then already invaded the Italian mainland. A republican Fascist regime was then set up under German control in northern Italy. This remained a German client state until the final collapse in 1945
6. M. le Lannou, *L'Europe et le Géographe*, Sciences Humaines et l'Intégration Européenne, College of Europe, Bruges, 1961
7. This essential unity of the Rhinelands was stressed by Mackinder in the early part of the century. *See* Halford Mackinder, *The Rhine*, London, 1908
8. This was a phrase coined by René Mayer who, with Jean Monnet, Robert Marjolin, Hervé Alphand and others, worked in the 1940s on the idea of European economic integration
9. The German desire for total possession had also been endowed with a romantic quality in Becker's 'Wacht am Rhein' and other patriotic songs. *Deutschen Rhein* was also intimately associated with many of the old Teutonic legends. France had formerly regarded the Rhine as one of her *limites naturelles*, but by the later nineteenth century Strasbourg had also come to be endowed with a symbolic quality denoting France's right to be there. The wreath of *immortelles* draped around the statue of Strasbourg after 1871 is testimony to the French emotionalism on this question. *See* Chapter 6
10. *See* Chapter 2, note 1
11. J. Lukacs, *Decline and Rise of Europe*, Westport, 1976
12. Switzerland is also a part of this in the physical sense and is also historically, culturally and economically closely bound up with her neighbours to the north. The only sense in which this is not true is the political one, arising from the policy of neutrality which the Swiss have maintained since the Helvetic confederacy was first established in the sixteenth century. Nevertheless, it has acted as host to numerous international bodies, the most famous having been the League of Nations at Geneva. (*See also* Chapter 6, note 6)
13. 'Yesterday the Rhine, our river, was a barrier, a frontier, a battleline . . . Today the Rhine can resume its natural and historical role. It can become a western bond'. General de Gaulle speaking in Strasbourg, 1945
14. 'General de Gaulle wanted [Europe] to stretch from the Atlantic to the Urals but thought of the Strait of Dover as an insuperable barrier . . .' (Y. Fouéré, *Towards a Federal Europe*, Swansea, 1980)

Chapter 5

Community Europe as a geopolitical unit

The assumption by the European Community of the role of spearhead in
the movement towards European unification was a major feature of
European internationalism in the years which followed World War II. Its
manifest, if restricted, success after centuries of statist political fragmenta-
tion has been attributed to various causes. Its continuing resilience, despite
the severe strains put upon it and a widespread feeling of dissatisfaction
with its performance, is in itself a phenomenon of importance. Political
analysts have seen the causes of this success both in the inherently regional
approach and in the advantages of limited functionalism. There is also the
acknowledged importance of the chronological element in producing for a
limited period of time a coincidence of optimum conditions, the right
international 'soup' for the birth of a new structure. The changed geopolitical situation after World War II had also profoundly affected Europe's
world position and this made international cooperation for the first time, a
favoured option. Western Europe's geographical structure, and in particular that of the central quadrilateral, provided the physical underpinning for
this. The character of this spatial dimension will now be further examined
in order to assess the extent to which the Community arises from a logic
founded in the nature of its territory.

It was seen in Chapter 3 that the member states themselves have their
own clearly identifiable spatial structures, which have resulted from and
contributed to the other elements of which they are constituted. These
structures subsequently facilitated the entrenchment of the states as the
primary units of geopolitical organization in Europe. Willingness by the
states to embark upon Community-type integration varied negatively with
the degree of congruence with the spatial model. It has been seen that
overall congruence with the basic model varied in the member states from
as high as 100 per cent to as low as 30 per cent. Non-congruence is not in
this context an entirely negative attribute, since it relates positively to the
existence of transnational spatial structures. By analogy with the importance of the spatial structures of the states, the long-term stability of the
Community cannot but be ensured by the existence of a discrete spatial
structure, so giving it a permanence above the vicissitudes of popular
attitudes and national policies.

The shape of the state in the normative model is as compact as possible, with its capital somewhere near the centre. There should be an absence of major internal barriers to communication and the internal physical arrangements should facilitate rather than prevent high levels of internal transaction. Most of the member states have tended to proximate to these characteristics, often by gradual territorial adjustments over long periods of time. The Community, however, does not conform well in its shape to this model. From the Hebrides off the north-west coast of Scotland to the Dodecanese in the eastern Aegean is a distance of some 3600 km, while from the Bay of Biscay to the nearest point on the Iron Curtain is under 1000 km. There are a number of breaks in physical continuity along the north-west to south-east axis, significant among them being the Irish Sea, the English Channel, the Alps and the Strait of Otranto. The largest contiguous low-lying area is the North Sea Lowland, which forms the western end of the North European Plain[1]. It includes the Aquitaine and Paris basins, the lower Rhinelands and Lowland Britain. It covers around 500 000 km^2, one-third of the total area of the Community, and is traversed by the rivers Elbe, Weser, Rhine, Seine, Loire, Garonne, Thames, Severn and Trent, all of which have been important historic lines of communication. It is bounded to the south by the Pyrenees and the Hercynian mountains from the Massif Central through to the Zwischengebirge, and in the north-west by the mountains of upland Britain from Cornwall to the Scottish Highlands. Gaps following the Rhône–Sâone, Loire, Garonne, Elbe, Severn and some smaller rivers link the Northern Sea Lowlands with areas of variable relief beyond. The Lowland and its associated Hercynian upland is terminated in the south by the Alps themselves, beyond which the natural conditions are quite different. Here are found the high mountains interspersed with relatively small and isolated areas of lowland which characterize the Mediterranean countries. In terms of human potential the Northern Sea Lowland has historically been rich in both agriculture and commerce, and has been able to support a relatively dense settlement. The uplands and more negative areas which form a great discontinuous arc around it are, in contrast, relatively lightly populated. In the Mediterranean regions of the Community the situation is demographically quite the reverse. Small densely populated lowland areas are separated from one another by large stretches of empty mountain country and by such seas as the Tyrrhenian, Ionian and Aegean. The Northern Sea Lowland has consequently a far greater built-in physical potential for human interaction as a result of the inherently diffusive possibilities of geographical contiguity. This is clearly observed in its leading role in the creation of the Community.

On the question of territoral organization, the centre–periphery structure is an intrinsic feature of the model. This has been identified, to a greater or lesser degree, in every member state of the Community. It has been seen that the genesis of the Community was closely associated with the territory of the historic Lotharingia and more particularly with the 'industrial Lotharingia' which arose earlier in the century. This industrial power-house was the focus of Community dynamics in the 1950s and one of its principal *raisons d'être*. Since then the situation has considerably changed, and this area, the Heavy Industrial Triangle, has lost much of its significance. With the energy revolution which has been taking place since the 1960s, the Triangle, although still producing half of EC(10)'s coal, is now responsible for only a quarter of its energy output. The output of the Triangle as a proportion of the Community's total energy consumption has now fallen to some 10 per cent[2]. The centre of indigenous energy production has now decisively moved northwards to the North Sea Energy Basin, which stretches from eastern Britain across the shallow continental shelf to northern Germany. This area is rich in oil, natural gas and coal, and is now responsible for some three-quarters of the Community's total energy production and for one-third of its consumption.

Likewise the relative importance of the Triangle's steel industry has declined considerably. In the 1950s it was still responsible for over three-quarters of the total steel output of the EC(6), but now it is down to around two-thirds of EC(6) and only a little over a half of that of the EC(10) as a whole. Much modern integrated iron and steel plant has been located elsewhere and, for reasons of costs, the North Sea and Mediterranean coasts have been of particular importance in the growth and modernization of the steel industry since the 1960s.

As a consequence of these new developments, the old coal- and steel-based heavy industrial core has been tending to break up, but it has not yet dissipated entirely. Rather, a wider and more diversified industrial region has come into existence, centring on the delta and the lower Rhinelands. Within this region heavy industry has tended to move towards the coasts, which are now the most economic locations having regard to the import of energy and raw materials; the growth of secondary manufacturing industry has been associated with the large urban areas of the Low Countries and the Rhinelands. The progressive occlusion of the frontiers from the 1950s had the effect of making this into a very central area in relation to the emerging transnational unit. The coming together of its previously separated component parts has produced a region of considerable economic strength. Taking the criteria of density of population, proportion of the labour force in industry, energy consumption and highest per capita GDPs, then it is possible to identify a large transnational area extending from the delta southwards into the Rhinelands. It contains the economic core regions of Belgium, the Netherlands and West Germany, which run over into each other to form a largely contiguous transnational urban region. Kormoss has identified a European metropolitan area[3] with many of the characteristics in embryo of the 'megalopolis'[4] of the eastern seaboard of the United States, and Clark delimited a 'central' region based on population potentials[5]. The possible effects of unity are well illustrated by Clark's 'before and after' maps, which show population potentials first in relation to the states and then to the Community as a whole. Clark's central region interestingly corresponds quite closely to Mackinder's 'great capital of the Rhinelands', which included Amsterdam, Rotterdam, Ghent, Brussels, Antwerp, Liège and Cologne[6].

By synthesizing a number of different criteria it is possible to identify a pre-eminent region which possesses on a continental scale many of the sort of criteria associated with the national core regions themselves. This transnational core is located astride that central frontier zone, the potential of which in the past was undermined both by its compartmentalization and

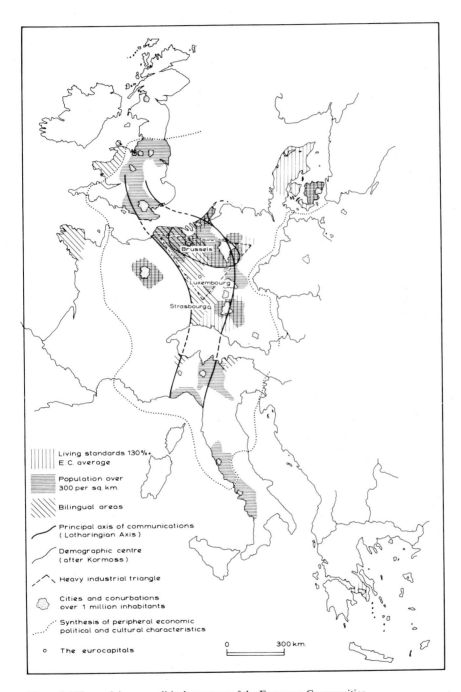

Living standards 130%+
E.C. average

Population over
300 per sq. km.

Bilingual areas

Principal axis of communications
(Lotharingian Axis)

Demographic centre
(after Kormoss)

Heavy industrial triangle

Cities and conurbations
over 1 million inhabitants

Synthesis of peripheral economic
political and cultural characteristics

o   The eurocapitals

0   300 km.

Brussels

Luxembourg

Strasbourg

Figure 5.1 The evolving geopolitical structure of the European Communities

its strategic vulnerability. It is significant that it centres on the northern part of Lotharingia, the old Middle Kingdom, and includes much of the Heavy Industrial Triangle which had so dominated the industrial strength and the geopolitical thinking of the countries of the central quadrilateral during the first half of the present century (*Figure 5.1*).

Conversely to this tendency to convergence at the centre, the peripheries of the member states, if examined together, can be seen to constitute a discontinuous ring around the edges of the Community. This continental periphery is widest in the west and south, where it stretches in a great arc from the west of the British Isles and France around to the Mediterranean islands, the Mezzogiorno and Greece (*Figure 5.1*). It is significant that peripheral characteristics are far less evident in the east, with the notable exception of the *Zonenrandgebiet* produced by the particular conditions prevailing along the Iron Curtain. The European periphery is characterized, on the whole, by the opposite conditions from those identified in the central regions – a high proportion of the workforce in agriculture and primary industry, a relatively small and sometimes insignificant tertiary sector and lower per capita energy consumption and per capita GDPs. There are migratory outflows of population and resources mainly towards the centre. Non-conformity of the peripheries with that overall national homogeneity characteristic of the states spills over the frontiers to create large transnational areas in which identification with the nation state is weak. This is a particular feature of what is frequently referred to as 'Celtic' Europe, which consists of the western parts of the British Isles together with Brittany[7]. To a degree also there are similar 'Mediterranean' cultural identifications in the islands and peninsulas on the Community's southern fringes.

The implications of the existence of this transnational periphery with its overlapping characteristics, relationships and problems is that those areas within it often have more in common with one another than they have with the states within which they are located. Despite constant protestations to the contrary, it is in the nature of the national core regions, and of the 'inner states'[8] adjunct to them, to seek to maintain their positions of pre-eminence. On the other hand, it is in the collective interest of the countries and regions which constitute the periphery to bring about a fundamental redistribution of wealth and power in their favour. The voice of the periphery has been added to other voices of underprivilege and hardship within the Community, and they have together been slowly translated into mechanisms for the transfer of resources to the peripheries as well as to other poorer regions and economic sectors.

A centre–periphery structure on a European scale can thus be identified, but the transnational European core nevertheless lacks the functional completeness associated with the core region of the mature state. This is especially noticeable in the fields of political decision-making, finance, dissemination of information and intellectual and cultural activity. The fact is that the European macrocore's pre-eminence is almost entirely demographic and industrial, while the national cores are multifunctional and have come to control most of the higher functions of the state. In this context the macrocore is as yet at an early stage of development; one could expect it to accrue more functions in time if the Community continues to evolve.

When analysing the changes which had taken place in the spatial structures of the member states, and particularly in the more advanced of them, it was observed that the characteristic annular core has in recent times tended to be replaced by a linear one following a major internal line of communications. In the context of the analysis of the spatial structure of the Community as a whole and the similarities which may or may not exist with national structures, the Rhine from the sea to the Alpine foreland resembles this kind of axis. It and its tributaries form a transnational connecting link between some of the major cities and conurbations in the Community. With the decline in the hold of the Heavy Industrial Triangle, major industrial activities, as has been seen, tended to extend to the north and south of it. The Rhine has, of course, been a major historical line of communication, but its importance was lessened by the deliberate distortion of communications systems in order better to serve the cause of autarchic nationalism. The existence of the Community has reinstated the Rhine axis to its key role in the communications system of the countries of the central quadrilateral. A wider 'Lotharingian axis'[9] has also been identified from the Rhine delta to northern Italy. Into this feed other lines of communication, notably the Rhône–Saône, Po, Main–Danube and the *börde* route along the northern edge of the Mittelgebirge.

This wider concept of a transnational linear core also has a relationship with Britain. Britain's decline from a major global power of the 1950s to an ailing European power of the 1980s has been accompanied by many internal spatial changes. Underlying these has been a marked change of orientation from west to east, from Atlantic Britain to European Britain.

Churchill's prognosis of the 1950s that Europe would always come second to 'the open sea' so far as the British were concerned proved by the 1970s to be quite false. The connecting link in the new, or at least reactivated, continental relationship is the south-east quadrant of the country, and this area has been proposed as part of a widely drawn European core region, more appropriate to the EC(10) as a whole. This had been enshrined in Wise's 'Golden Triangle', with its apexes in Birmingham, Paris and the Ruhr[10]. Kormoss enlarged his European 'megalopolis' north and west into Britain and Eriplan's 'core area' includes also the south-east region of England[11]. The essential thinking behind these and other similar concepts is that Lowland Britain is but a discontinuous part of the adjacent Continent, and that the two sides of the Channel have more to unite than to divide them. This had been expressed by Halford Mackinder before World War I when he wrote of 'a great plain, low-lying, fertile, free from long winter frosts, free from summer droughts, densely populated and traversed by slow navigable rivers which are entered by the tides. A shallow channel, tideswept, extends through the centre of that plain so that one section of it, the plain of southern England, is superficially detached from the remainder, namely the plain of northern France, the Netherlands and north Germany. But within all its parts it presents the same conditions for the development of human societies, saving only the insularity of Britain'[12]. The transformation of this relationship into contemporary human terms suggests an extension of the 'Lotharingian axis' across the Channel (*Figure 5.1*). The Thames–Pennine 'coffin' is the obvious line of this extension, so as to include virtually the whole of the British economic core region. An axial belt extending from the Irish Sea to the shores of the Mediterranean includes the economic core regions of six of the member states, together with the capital cities of five of them. It has the densest and most advanced communications network and the most accessible nodes in relation to the Community as a whole. It has a large number of the Community's 'euroports', a high proportion of the industrialized areas and the largest contiguous area of high per capita GDPs. Many of the major changes and developments in Europe's economic geography since the 1950s have been on and around this extended axis. They include south-east England, the composite delta, the middle Rhinelands, the sub-Alpine regions of Germany, France and Italy and the western Mediterranean coastlands. Unlike an annular core which grows endogenously, a linear core extends exogenously, and so penetrates towards erstwhile peripheral regions, transforming their situation in relation to the structures of the Community as a whole.

The central axial belt, or Atlantic–Mediterranean axis, connects together Europe's major economic and political power centres and includes the locations of the Community's own executive and decision-making institutions. In its Lotharingian central section it follows that shatter-belt of internal frontiers and the Franco–Germanic language divide which, until very recently, was very much an area of contention rather than cooperation. It is crossed by the physical barriers of the Channel and the Alps which also, in modern times, have divided rather than united the peoples living on either side of them. The progressive occlusion of the frontiers, together with the retreat of language-based nationalism in the states, has given modern technology a freer rein in the development of new forms of communication. This, in turn, has provided the infrastructure for the emergence of a functioning and interdependent European linear core.

Another important characteristic of the mature state is the high degree of homogeneity likely to develop in a population group which has lived in a particular territory for a long period of time. This homogeneity is deemed to convert a population group into a nation. Predominant national groups of this sort characterize all but one of the member states of the Community, and this situation naturally implies an absence of homogeneity at Community level. This is reflected in the variety of languages, cultures and historical experiences to be found throughout the Community. There exist also a number of wider cultural identifications, such as Anglo-Saxon throughout the British Isles, Celtic along the western fringes and Francophone in the western half of the central quadrilateral. The Latin–Germanic divide already alluded to, a major cultural fault line since the age of Charlemagne, spills over the boundaries of the Community south into Switzerland.

Historically such state and supra-state identifications have proved divisive and have contributed to conflict in Europe. However, over long periods major European political and intellectual movements have affected large areas of the continent with little relationship to contemporary state frontiers. Such movements have given a unity to the European experience, which transcends those particularist identifications encouraged by the states. Major pan-European movements which have in turn influenced large parts of the territory of the Community during the past

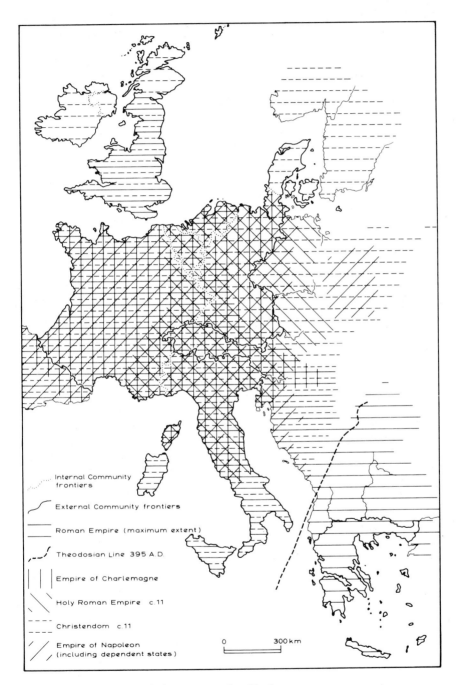

Internal Community frontiers

External Community frontiers

Roman Empire (maximum extent)

Theodosian Line 395 A.D.

Empire of Charlemagne

Holy Roman Empire c.11

Christendom c.11

Empire of Napoleon (including dependent states)

0   300 km

Figure 5.2 Historical factors in the common cultural heritage

2000 years are the Roman, Holy Roman, Carolingian and Napoleonic Empires and western Christendom (*Figure 5.2*). These all brought with them the idea of a wider European polity, and they became the vehicles for the dissemination of common ideas in political organization, law, culture, art, architecture and religion. None of them ever covered the whole of the territory of the present Community, but all ten members have been affected by at least one of them. Their collective incidence has been greatest in the countries of the quadrilateral together with northern Italy. The influence of every one of them has been felt in a zone extending from the western part of the Rhine delta southwards as far as Rome. Their collective incidence lessens towards the peripheries, and Ireland and Denmark, while both members of Christendom, were never part of any of the four great pan-European empires. Britain, southern Italy and the eastern fringes of the German Federal Republic were each within two of the five and Greece was within the territory of the Roman Empire only. From the Theodosian division[13] of the Empire in the fourth century, this home of European civilization came within the eastern Byzantine world, and it was not again to develop close ties with the West until the present century.

The legacy of the unity arising from the pan-European movements began to give place after the Renaissance to national identifications. Territorial units, enclosed by increasingly impermeable frontiers, came to be worshipped with a quasi-religious fervour. Despite the residue of Christianity, admittedly very divided on doctrine, and the clear memory of a classical cultural unity expressed through Latin and Greek, the states steadily grew apart politically, economically and culturally, and 'my nation, right or wrong' became the prevailing political philosophy. It was the divisiveness implicit in all this which led the continent inexorably towards the shattering internecine wars of the first half of the twentieth century. This, in turn, facilitated the process of unification through the drastic weakening of the states which then took place. It also allowed the curtains to be opened so as to reveal the historic European heritage, transmitted from the cultures of the ancient eastern Mediterranean, which, like Europe's geopolitical structure, had been concealed beneath the polychromatic states.

While until after World War II the states operated in considerable isolation from one another, in the more advanced parts of the continent there had been a tendency to the emergence of common characteristics which were later reinforced by the subsequent moves to unity. Among the more important of these were industrialization, urbanization, modernization, material affluence, pluralism and the Protestant and secular traditions (*Figure 5.3*). The highest incidence of these particular characteristics is in a wide zone stretching from southern Britain to northern Italy. They are all to be found around the south of the North Sea, together with adjacent parts of the Rhinelands. Their overall incidence is weakest in the north-western British Isles, southern Italy and Greece.

While a large number of transnational similarities of a historical, cultural and economic character can be identified, the national systems, expressed in their languages, remain paramount as immediate influences on the attitudes of the Community's 260 million people. Education, information,

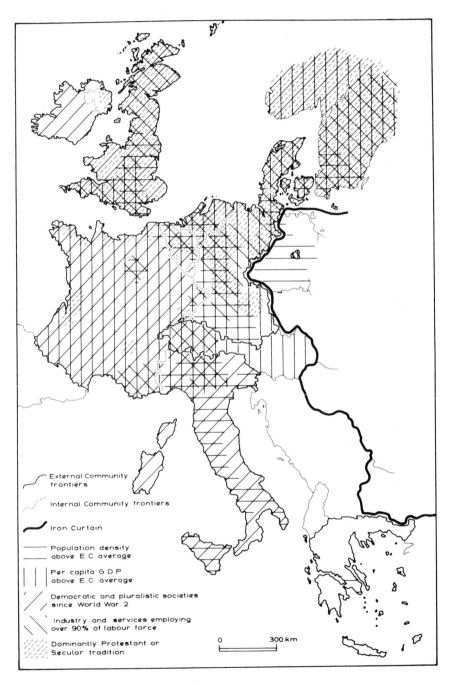

Figure 5.3 Contemporary transnational features

publishing, the arts and television all use first and foremost the national languages as means of communication and they combine to form powerful cocoons within which the population group functions. Compared with this, 'European' cultural influences remain relatively peripheral in their effects. English, French and German, the three dominant languages, are also the linguistic vehicles for large transnational cultures which operate both within and outside the Community itself. Each is spoken by around 60 million people within the Community, as also is the fourth language, Italian. Unlike the other three, however, Italian is no longer an important international language[14].

In Europe as a whole, the most important of these languages is German, which is spoken as a first language by around 90 million people on either side of the Iron Curtain. It is understood by many millions more in the East European countries, for long under the hegemony of one or other of the two Germanic empires of *Mitteleuropa*. From a global point of view the most important of the European languages is now undoubtedly English, which is the first language of over 300 million people. Two-thirds of them are in the United States of America and English is now without rival as the principal *lingua franca* of the Western world. It is since World War II, and largely as a consequence of it, that it has come to the fore in Western Europe. This situation arose out of the joint Anglo-American hegemony in Western Europe throughout the post-war years, and it was later consolidated by the dominant position of English in the areas of Western influence in the world at large. Since the 1950s it has become the principal second language in all the non-English-speaking members of the Community, and the most frequently used vehicle for official international communication. In many ways it has already reached the position of being the Community's *lingua franca*.

However, the English language also carries with it an Anglo-American culture of popular music, mass-appeal films, fast food and casual dress which has, since the 1960s, seduced a large part of the youth of Europe and beaten the indigenous cultures hands down in the battle for their hearts, minds and pockets. Its triumph has been eased by its exposure on radio and television networks throughout the Community. It is, of course, Atlantic rather than European, and its triumph is a cultural and, through this, also an economic consequence of the ascendancy of the maritime world over the old Europe. The idea of accepting the primacy of the language of cultural colonization, especially since the Community was itself a reaction to other forms of American penetration in the 1950s, goes against the grain for many Europeans.

The most vocal opponents of American domination in whatever form have, since the 1950s, been the French, who have taken up the cudgels for what they regard as being a more truly European Europe. In the 1960s Britain was condemned by de Gaulle as a 'Trojan horse' for the penetration of American influence and is still seen by many as a staging-post in the advance of American Coca Cola imperialism. Implicit in the French strategy from the beginning was the rejection of the influence of *les anglo-saxons* and its replacement by a Franco–German *entente*. It was also implicit in French thinking that the language of the new Europe should be French, which had been the *lingua franca* of the educated classes from the

Atlantic to the Urals since the seventeenth century. Although still spoken by 60 million people as a first language in Europe and as a principal second language by nearly double that number – ironically, most of them in the British Isles, the home of Anglo-Saxon civilization – French rapidly lost ground to English after World War II. In spite of this, the francophones claim that since English is now a world rather than a European language, true Europeanism can more appropriately be expressed through the medium of French.

A further characteristic of the mature state is the relatively high level of internal transactions of all sorts as compared with those conducted with Third World countries. The degree to which the Community is developing this characteristic is seen in the changes which have taken place in the foreign trade patterns of the member countries. Over a half of the total international trade of the ten members is now conducted with other member countries. On the basis of total populations, this represents a trade weighting in favour of the Community of 4:1 as compared with the rest of the Western (class 1) countries and of 9:1 in favour of the Community as compared with all third countries. The change which this demonstrates in the international trading patterns of the member countries is seen in the fact that in 1957 the intra-Community trade of the EC(6) countries represented some 30 per cent of their world total, and Britain's trade with the Community countries in that year represented only 13 per cent of hers. As a proportion of their total international trade, intra-EC(10) trade has nearly doubled over this period. In the individual member states the proportions still vary considerably, from the United Kingdom's 40 per cent to BLEU's 70 per cent. The proportion of intra-EC trade conducted by the countries of EC(6) is generally higher than that of the newer members, but the latter have been catching up fast. Ireland now actually conducts over three-quarters of its trade within the Community, the highest proportion of the ten member countries.

The importance of intra-Community transactions is also to be seen in the trade of the great ports, especially those at the continental termini of the central axial belt. These ports carry a large proportion of Europe's maritime trade and their hinterlands are transnational. Those of the composite delta, Rotterdam, Amsterdam and Antwerp, extend deep into the Rhinelands, while on the Mediterranean, Marseille-Etang de Berre, Genoa, Venice and Trieste all handle goods destined for transalpine Europe. The total goods traffic of these 'euroports' is around 600 million tonnes per annum, and this represents about one-third of the total external goods traffic of the member countries.

The international movement of labour is another important element in internal transaction. In 1968 it was completely freed from restriction in the countries of the EC(6), but long before this a considerable movement had already been taking place within the Community in response to the differential levels of economic growth in the 1950s. By far the most significant intra-Community movement of this kind was that from Italy to West Germany, and by the early 1970s there were over 600 000 Italians working in the latter's industrial areas[15]. Central to this was the movement of labour from the poorest region in the EC(6) – the Italian Mezzogiorno – to one of its richest, the middle Rhinelands. At the same time Italian workers found their way into the Benelux countries and other parts of north-west Europe, as indeed they had been doing since the earlier part of the century. There have been similar strong flows of Irish workers to Britain and during the 1950s of Greeks to West Germany and Benelux.

Basically these flows resolve themselves into a pattern of labour movement from the north-western and the south-eastern peripheries into the central areas of the Community, in particular to the quadrilateral and to the south-east quadrant of Britain. By the 1980s there were some one and three-quarter million expatriate Community workers living in other Community countries, and nearly half of these were living in West Germany and Benelux alone. If labour migration from third countries into the Community is also included, then this pattern is heavily reinforced. Large flows of workers have taken place from south-east Europe, in particular from Yugoslavia and Turkey, to West Germany and Benelux and from Spain and Portugal to France. Large numbers of Arab workers have also migrated to France, especially from Morocco, Algeria and Tunisia, the former French dependencies in the Maghreb.

These powerful intra-Community and extra-Community migratory flows have been further reinforced by intra-national movements. Notable internal migratory flows have taken place from the Mezzogiorno to the north of Italy, from western France to the Paris region, from the Iron Curtain fringes – and until 1962 from the German Democratic Republic itself – to the western parts of the Federal Republic and from the north-west to the south-east in Britain. These have had the overall effect of adding to the demographic and economic strength of the centre and lessening that of the peripheries. The only really significant labour migration from completely outside the Euro–Mediterranean area has been that to Britain. Like that into France from the Maghreb, this is the legacy of the days of overseas empire, and it has come mainly from the former dependent territories of the West Indies and the Indian subcontinent. The main recipients have been the large cities and conurbations, and especially London and the Midlands.

The most multi-national and multi-ethnic parts of the Community are the delta-Rhineland 'megalopolis' together with Paris and south-eastern Britain. This reinforces the multilingual character of the delta-Rhinelands, giving this area a high degree of linguistic, ethnic and cultural diversity. It consequently lacks that human homogeneity which has been identified as a characteristic of the mature state and is especially likely to be a feature of a national core area.

Another transactional movement of considerable importance is investment and establishment. The growth of multinational firms and the increasing geographical spread of their activities has been a characteristic feature of the period since World War II. Much of their activity has taken place on the territory of the Community, and it has developed both indigenously and exogenously. However, since the multinationals do not operate exclusively in the context of the Community alone it does not have its own multinational geography which can be examined and comprehended in isolation and without reference to developments elsewhere. If one is considering specifically the European multinationals, then at a minimum it is necessary to examine their activities in the whole of the

European maritime crescent. A large number of the most important European multinationals have their headquarters outside the Community itself, especially in Sweden and Switzerland. Companies from these and from other non-Community European countries have tended to establish themselves in the Community in response to the locational advantages of proximity to large markets for their products. The most favoured operating locations for these and for the intra-Community multinationals themselves are in the Benelux countries and in adjacent parts of the delta-Rhinelands. The suitability of this for establishment and investment relates to its centrality and to the facts that it is both multilingual and cosmopolitan, that in general it welcomes foreign investment and that it is close to the international decision-making centres which, sometimes quite irrationally, themselves exercise a powerful attraction. Other places where the activities of multinational companies are especially concentrated are the London and Paris regions.

Europe's peripheries have also been able to attract international investment and the establishment of multinational firms. This unlikely development is attributable to the much lower unit manufacturing costs than those in the more central regions, and also to the inducements provided both by the Community and by national governments. Community aid from a variety of sources including the ECSC, EAGGF[16], the Investment Bank and, of course, the Regional Fund itself, have collectively made a considerable impact on certain areas. The most important of these are Ireland – south and north – and the Mezzogiorno, into which since 1973 nearly a half of all funds have been channelled. The western parts of both Britain and France have also been beneficiaries. However, geographical remoteness from markets, lack of infrastructural development and even security dangers in places have frequently weighed against the financial inducements and curtailed the scale of development.

ι One indicator of the attractiveness of particular European countries and regions to international capital and establishment is the geographical pattern of United States investment in the territory of the Community. It has been said that the Americans are really the best Europeans since only they can really look beyond national frontiers to view the continent as a whole, at least in economic terms. The largest recipients of American capital investment since World War II have been the United Kingdom and West Germany. ι France has had less and Italy a much smaller share. An examination of the distribution of American investment per capita reveals the countries of Benelux are at the top, followed by the United Kingdom and West Germany. The Republic of Ireland is also high, but France and Italy are again lower down. More specifically, it is apparent that there is a high concentration of American investment in the delta-Rhinelands and in adjacent south-east Britain. Outside this extended area only the Paris region has a high total.

A final attribute of the mature state is the extent to which it is bounded by impermeable or 'hard' frontiers which effectively ring it as a discrete area of human activity. Physically, as has been seen, the Community is far from constituting a compact or coherent unit. The central quadrilateral apart, it is physically very diverse and is cut by major barriers to easy surface communication (*Figure 5.4*). In spite of this, its external physical

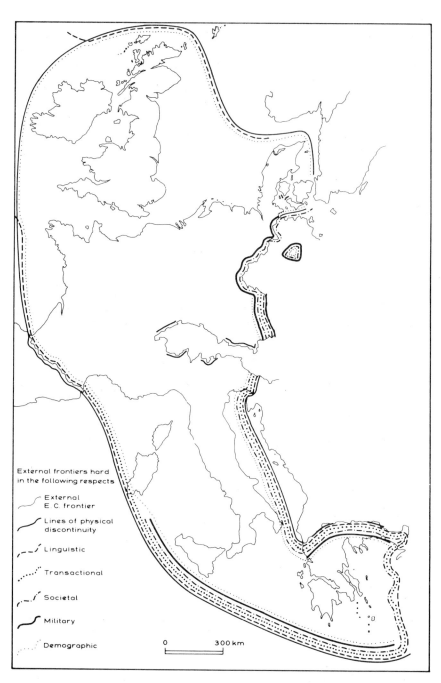

Figure 5.4 Characteristics of the external frontiers

boundaries are more clear-cut. In ancient times the Mediterranean Sea unified its riparian lands but, since the Islamic conquests of over a thousand years ago, it has separated population groups of a very different character ethnically, politically, economically and culturally. These economic differences have tended to become greater in modern times as a result of the great advances which have taken place in Europe. To the west the huge width of the Atlantic makes it a natural divide and to the north Scandinavia is physically discontinuous. In the heart of the Community the Alps have been a prerequisite of Switzerland's long-standing independence and neutrality by making it so inaccessible to the surrounding powers. Only eastwards across the north European plain is there a contiguous and physically open frontier, and this has historically been a major routeway linking the peoples of the west with those of the east of the continent. The fact that the contacts along it have frequently been of an unwelcome kind is one of the underlying *raisons d'être* of the Community itself.

In matters of language and culture it has been seen that, while there is a great diversity within the Community, there is overspill across the external frontiers. The western fringes, and especially the British Isles, have close cultural and linguistic links with the maritime world as a whole and especially with North America. French cultural ties with the Canadian province of Quebec and with her former African dependencies have also remained strong and they have been deliberately fostered as part of a global Francophone policy. The area of German speech and culture, the *sprachboden* and the *culturboden*[17], spills across the North European Plain into Eastern Europe and over the Alps to the Danube valley. As has been observed, German is the most widely spoken language in Europe after Russian. Denmark has historically looked east and north, and she has close cultural relationships with the other Nordic countries. Thus only to the south is there, culturally speaking, a hard shell, that following the Mediterranean and separating the European from the Arab worlds. Ironically, two thousand years ago it was the routeway for the dissemination of Middle Eastern civilization to Europe.

Contacts between the Community and the non-Community extensions of western Europe to the north-east and the south-west are close. This is especially true of Scandinavia, the more highly developed of the two and the one which is most akin to the Community's north-west European heartland. The Danish archipelago is in a variety of ways an important link between the two, and transactions in the areas of trade, investment and industrial establishment are all at high levels. Transactions of this kind are even greater with Switzerland and Austria which, interposed as they are between the north and the south of the Community, handle increasing amounts of intra-Community traffic across their territories. This traffic has greatly increased as a consequence of Italy's orientation to the north together with the expansion of the cisalpine euroports. Both of these countries, together with Scandinavia and Portugal, are members of the European Free Trade Association, and, under agreements negotiated in the early 1970s, they have industrial free trade arrangements with the Community. In the Communist world, the German Democratic Republic has been granted free access to the market of the German Federal Republic. This situation has arisen out of the Federal Republic's insistence that, although there are two German states, there is only one German nation, and imports from East Germany are actually deemed to be part of internal German trade.

A final attribute of the hardness of the frontiers arises from the political systems of the neighbouring states. Those to the south across the Mediterranean and to the east on the other side of the Iron Curtain have quite different attitudes and traditions, and most of them do not come near to the democratic pluralism which is the underlying Community political ideal. From this viewpoint these frontiers are therefore hard ones. In contrast to this, the countries of the Alps and Scandinavia have virtually identical political systems, and, in respect of this attribute, their frontiers with the Community are as a consequence very soft.

An overall synthesis of these physical, cultural, economic and political characteristics reveals very hard frontiers facing the Mediterranean and the Balkan peninsula (*Figure 5.4*). These completely contrast with the very soft frontiers with Scandinavia and the Alpine countries. The Iron Curtain, which has, since the late 1940s, been the principal scene of the 'eyeball to eyeball' superpower confrontation, is, on the basis of the criteria examined here, in reality softer than the Mediterranean frontier. This situation results from the physical and cultural overlapping of the intra-German frontier and the economic softening which has occurred as a result of increases in transactions across it. It is the natural softness of this frontier which has necessitated its being sustained by massive military power emanating from Europe's antagonistic extended peripheries[18]. At the other side of the Community the 'Atlantic corridor' carries the close relationship between Western Europe and North America, institutionalized since the late 1940s in such organizations as OECD and NATO.

Yet, in spite of the strength of the Western and Eastern contacts, as a geopolitical region bounded by relatively hard frontiers it is Europe's maritime crescent as a whole stretching from Scandinavia to the eastern Mediterranean which comes out more strongly even than the Community itself.

To what extent, then, does it appear that the European Community reproduces in macrocosm the state characteristics as described in the normative model? In physical terms, the great north-west to south-east extent and the internal physical barriers do not facilitate ease of communication between the central and the peripheral regions. Yet it has been possible to identify the emergence of a central axial belt, a multilinear and multifunctional axis of surface communications linking the major centres of population and industry from the Irish Sea to the shores of the Mediterranean (*Figure 5.1*). It is in the delta-Rhinelands, the central part of this axis, that pan-European influences have been historically most in evidence and where territorial nationalism has been at its weakest. With the decrease in that divisiveness associated with nationalism, a marked transfrontier unity has begun to emerge. The area is multilingual, and since the 1950s has become also multi-ethnic, but French has the ascendancy as the principal international *lingua franca*. It is historically, economically and politically the heartland of the Community itself, and the germinal area of the Community idea and its implementation.

In contrast to this, towards the Community's peripheries local and national particularisms remain much more in evidence, and the sense of being 'European' is generally far weaker. As for internal transactions, it has been seen that these have increased considerably since the 1950s and far more rapidly than those between the Community and Third World countries. However, the external frontiers are not as a consequence uniformly hard, and those with the rest of maritime Europe are more often likely to be very soft.

The Community as a whole does indeed conform to a number of the characteristics of the spatial model in Chapter 2. There is the centre–periphery spatial structure and the central axis and its associated territories which forms the 'inner state' in terms of the modified model (*Figure 3.3*). Associated with this there are the high and steadily increasing levels of internal transaction using a variety of methods of communication which have been developed and improved upon since the 1950s. In contrast, the scores are far lower in physical unity and frontier impermeability, and there is considerable cultural and linguistic diversity. Taking a synthesis of all the major groups of characteristics, it is the quadrilateral which comes out with the highest degree of homogeneity in virtually all ways. Of all the characteristics which have been mentioned, it is only in language and religion that important variations now exist within this area. Closely associated with it and sharing a large number of common characteristics are the physically separated parts of the central axial belt in the south-east of Britain and the north-west of Italy. The most typical characteristics of advanced Western societies are to be found along the transalpine sections of the central axial belt and in the areas immediately adjacent to the east of it. In contrast to the west and south of it, these characteristics are in evidence to a far less extent.

The single most salient feature of the spatial structure of the Community appears to be the relative strength and homogeneity of the more central areas in contrast to the greater weakness and diversity of the western and southern peripheries. The quadrilateral united by the Monnet-inspired Franco–German *entente* of the 1950s has been the political epicentre of all subsequent developments. It has continued to muster sufficient political will, internal cohesion and economic strength to form a hub holding together a far-flung diversity of countries, stretching now from the northern Atlantic to the Middle East. Had it not been for the consistency of this resolve at the centre it is extremely improbable that they themselves would have found it possible to set in train so grandiose and transnational a venture.

Notes

1. G. Parker, *The Logic of Unity*, 3rd edn, London, 1981
2. Total energy consumption of the EC(10) in 1981 was 987 million tonnes oe. Of this, indigenously produced coal accounted for only 247 million tonnes (172 million tonnes oe) and the Triangle for approximately 116 million tonnes
3. I. B. F. Kormoss, *Les Communautés Européennes: essai d'une carte de densité de population*, Bruges, 1959
4. J. Gottmann, *Megalopolis*, New York, 1961
5. C. Clark, F. Wilson and J. Bradley, 'Industrial Location and Economic Potential in Europe', *Regional Studies* No 3, 1969

6. Halford Mackinder, 'Geographical Conditions affecting the British Empire: the British Isles', *Geographical Journal* **33,** 1909

7. Only the extreme western fringes can now really with truth be called Celtic. Anglo-Saxon cultural and ethnic incursions have been considerable in Scotland, Wales and Ireland and the old Celtic languages of Manx and Cornish are long dead. The total number of Celtic speakers is now only about one and a half million – under 1 per cent of the population of EC(10) – and the overwhelming proportion of them are in Brittany and Wales alone

8. This concept is examined in Chapter 3

9. This term was first used by N. Despicht in 1969 in *The Common Transport Policy of the European Communities*, PEP, London, 1969. It has since been variously defined and has come to denote the concept of a central axis. See Parker, op. cit., Chapter 9

10. M. J. Wise 'The Common Market and the Changing Geography of Europe', *Geography* **XLVIII,** Part 2, 1963. See also P. Odell, 'London and the Golden Triangle', *New Society* **16,** 1970

11. J. Robert, 'Prospective Study on Physical Planning and the Environment in the Megalopolis in Formation in North-West Europe', *Urban Ecology* **I,** 1976

12. Mackinder, op. cit.

13. In AD 395 the Emperor Theodosius divided the Roman Empire, and the dividing line passed from north to south through modern Yugoslavia. The capital of the western half was Rome and that of the eastern half was Constantinople. From then on the western and eastern Roman traditions rapidly diverged

14. This is so despite the massive emigration which has taken place from Italy since the late nineteenth century. Most of this has gone to the United States and South America, but the Italians, coming late, were forced to adopt the languages of the countries into which they went

15. W. Bohning, *The Migration of Workers in the United Kingdom and the European Community*, Oxford, 1972

16. The European Agricultural Guidance and Guarantee Fund (EAGGF) was established in 1962 as an instrument of the Common Agricultural Policy. It was intended to assist in the modernization of the agricultural sector, to provide secure markets for producers and to ensure food supplies to consumers. The EAGGF now accounts for some two-thirds of the Community's annual budget, and by far the greater part is used for price guarantee. It has been instrumental in causing overproduction which has resulted in the infamous 'mountains' and 'lakes'. In spite of this it has made an important contribution to the transformation of European agriculture since the 1960s

17. The areas of German speech and German culture. A discussion of these terms and their distribution is found in Dickinson, *The German Lebensraum*, op. cit. He also examines the ideas of *Reichsboden* (the state) and *Volksboden* (the folk)

18. Here there is a clear difference between European and American attitudes. The Europeans, and especially the West Germans, are interested in 'softening' the frontier for political, strategic and economic reasons. West Germany's *ostpolitik* has been designed for this purpose. The Americans are more interested in shoring up the European glacis and ensuring the containment of the Soviet Union. The case of the natural gas pipeline from Siberia to Western Europe is an instance of this. The Europeans want and need it while the Americans regard the whole project with some suspicion

Chapter 6

The Eurocapitals: the roles of Strasbourg, Luxembourg and Brussels

In August 1949 the first meeting of the Consultative Assembly of the Council of Europe took place in the French city of Strasbourg, located in Alsace on the Rhine frontier with Germany. It was here that the first debates about the future of European unity took place and these were to lead, two years later, to the establishment of the first of the European Communities. The headquarters of this first Community was Luxembourg, and six years later the second and third Communities came into being with Brussels as their *chef lieu provisoire* (provisional capital). Thus by the end of the 1950s the three cities of Strasbourg, Luxembourg and Brussels had become the principal locations of EC executive, administrative and legal operations; they were the *de facto* Eurocapitals. Each one of them had reached this position as a result of specific historical and geographical circumstances.

It has been seen that the international situation in Western Europe during the first half of the present century was dominated by the hostility between France and Germany, a hostility which was in part the consequence of territorial disputes. Strasbourg, strategically located on 'the lip of the wound' and having been forced to change its nationality four times during the previous three-quarters of a century, more than anywhere else symbolized the conflict (*Figure 4.1*). To the Germans it had always been a German city, and they wished to reunite it, together with the whole of Alsace and eastern Lorraine, with the Fatherland. To the French it was one of the great ring of bastions defending the sacred hexagon's 'natural frontiers'. During the long period of German rule following the French defeat of 1871 the symbolic statue of Strasbourg in the Place de la Concorde was draped with a wreath of *immortelles* to demonstrate the grief and shame of the French nation. Then in 1949, after two further bloody Franco–German wars, this much fought-over city was to become the symbol of the dawn of a new era of cooperation. It was here in Strasbourg that the plans for the new Europe were first seriously debated.

The minute state of Luxembourg, only about the size of a French *département*, is likewise strategically located between France and Germany. It was this neutral position between the two antagonistic great powers, as well as its long tradition of steel-making, which made it an acceptable choice as headquarters of ECSC in 1952. In 1957 Luxembourg was also considered for the role of headquarters of the two new Communities, but there was little enthusiasm for this development within the Grand Duchy itself. While the Luxembourgers had welcomed ECSC, they were understandably less enthusiastic about the idea of another international organization being located on their small territory. There was considerable fear that it could result in the dilution of the special character of the Grand Duchy, a character which had been the justification for its independence over the years. So the choice of *chef lieu provisoire* fell to Brussels, which also possessed many of the other features judged to be desirable. These included its central and easily accessible location, and the fact that Belgium, although large compared with Luxembourg, is a relatively small state by European standards.

The three 'Eurocities' are very different from one another in both size and urban character, and their selection to be European Community headquarters was the result, in each case, of the perceived needs and circumstances of the times. Yet the three do have certain common features. It has been suggested that the fact that they are notable gastronomic centres would have had a particular attraction in the austere years following World War II. Be this as it may, there are also features of greater geopolitical relevance. One is that all three are either on or adjacent to the great Latin–Germanic linguistic divide. They are bilingual, with German and French being spoken both in Strasbourg and in Luxembourg, and Flemish and French in Brussels. The Grand Duchy of Luxembourg also has its old Germanic dialect of Letzeburgesch, and English is now widely spoken and understood in all three. All three are also within the territory of the ancient Lotharingia, and in that central frontier zone which has for centuries been the battleground for the vestigal lands of the Middle Kingdom. Since they were not integral and permanent parts of the great powers, they retained the germ of Europeanism to a greater extent than occurred in the national heartlands themselves. Since World War II, as has been seen, the movement towards European unity has totally transformed the relative position of these lands from one of peripherality in relation to the states to centrality in relation to the continent as a whole. The Eurocities, chosen in the late 1940s and 1950s because they were, so to speak, politically in the front line, have now become central in relation to the Community's emerging geopolitical structure.

Since they were first chosen there have been a number of changes in their respective roles. These changes began with the administrative merger of the three Communities in 1968 and the decision to locate the enlarged organization principally in Brussels. Thus after fifteen years Luxembourg ceased to be the headquarters of the ECSC, but it retained a number of functions which it had gained in the meantime, notably the Court and the executive of the European Parliament. Strasbourg remained the home of the quite independent Council of Europe, but the *Maison de l'Europe* was also to remain one of the meeting-places of the Parliament. Thus by the end of the 1960s Brussels had emerged as incontestably the most important of the Eurocities, and its wider international role was also strengthened by the transfer of the headquarters of NATO to it from Paris in 1968[1]. The most important business has come to be increasingly conducted in Brus-

sels, and the real significance of the other two has thus markedly diminished. They retain their more limited and specialized functions, and they remain 'Holy Places' in the iconography of the Community. This is particularly true of Luxembourg, with its close association with the two great pioneers of European unity, Monnet and Schuman, and it is also the place where the Community was first launched.

The dominant position which Brussels has attained among the Eurocapitals springs from a number of factors. Important amongst these is the continuing readiness of the Belgian government to encourage international organizations to use their capital as headquarters. There is also the clear advantage of location in a major metropolis. With a population of over one million, Brussels is one of the dozen largest cities in the Community, having four times the population of Strasbourg and ten times that of Luxembourg[2]. It is the only one of the three which is a capital city in the full sense, and has social and cultural services to match. Its communications network is by far the best of the three, and it is the most accessible from the rest of the Community (*Figure 6.1*). Accessibility by air is now vital for an international city, and with its large international airport Brussels is well connected to the other Community capitals. Ironically, the only important European cities with which it is not well connected by air are Luxembourg and Strasbourg.

Brussels is thus unquestionably the executive and administrative centre of the Community, although its official status remains a provisional one. However, the question of a single definitive headquarters has come up as a major issue since the first direct elections to the European Parliament in 1979. Officially, Parliament is supposed to hold its sessions in both Luxembourg and Strasbourg, but in 1980 the parliamentarians decided that the *Maison de l'Europe* in Strasbourg would be their normal meeting-place. This decision was come to partly on the grounds of convenience, but also because the French government had insisted for political reasons that Strasbourg must remain the headquarters of the Parliament. The problem is only temporarily resolved, because Luxembourg still lays claim to being the meeting-place, and the Parliamentary executive has to shuttle back and forth from the Luxembourg headquarters. It has been generally agreed that this *Europaïsche Wanderzirkus* (European travelling circus) is costly and unsatisfactory, and that Parliament and its staff should be definitively located in a single place[3]. The problem lies in agreeing where this should be. Each of the Eurocities would be a possibility, and there are pressure groups in favour of each of them.

Those in favour of Strasbourg led, as one might expect, by the French government, point to the city's symbolic significance in the process of Franco–German reconciliation, and more practically to the magnificent *Palais de l'Europe*[4], which was completed in 1978. Those in favour of Luxembourg point to the fact that it is already an important Community city, the home of the European Investment Bank, the Court, the Statistical Office and one of the European Schools. Most relevant of all is the fact that it is the location of Parliament's own permanent secretariat. The Luxembourg government has long given up its earlier objections to Community activity on its territory. In pursuance of the aim of attracting Parliament to settle there, a grandiosely conceived assembly hall was completed in 1980 next door to the secretariat on the Kirchberg site.

The arguments in favour of moving the Parliament to Brussels need to be less strenuously pursued, since they stem from the thinking which led to the Community's activities being increasingly located in that city in the first place. It is maintained that to ensure the maximum efficacy, and to carry out its functions of scrutiny, Parliament needs to be in close proximity to the two major decision-making bodies, the Council and the Commission. To promote ease of contacts the three principal institutions should therefore be located in one place on the model of a national capital city.

This is regarded in many quarters as being not just a matter of the re-location of an existing institution but of making better provision for what could well become a more significant part of the Community's decision-making structure. The question of the permanent site for such an institution is thus politically very important. It naturally ties in closely with the whole question of the establishment of a permanent capital city which would implicitly recognize the political dimension of the Community.

The function of a capital city is generally considered to be more than merely that of being the seat of government. It has also an iconographical one, enshrining the physical expression of the self-image of a people and perhaps also being a palimpsest of their history[5]. As to the suitability of any city to perform this kind of role in Europe, one would naturally think of Rome or – a long way behind – Charlemagne's ancient capital of Aachen. Most of the great cities of modern Europe have a national rather than a European iconographical heritage[6]. Since World War II it is only the three Eurocities which have developed a strong association with the idea of Europe in the popular mind. In addition to the advantages which Brussels possesses, it has a head-start because the major decision-making apparatus is already there, and it would be a daunting task to justify its transfer elsewhere without there being very good reasons indeed. In addition to this, for two decades a multiplicity of international and multinational organizations – banks, firms, corporations, pressure groups, unions – have set up in the city on the strength of its acting as host to the Community's executive and decision-making institutions. As this process has continued, Brussels has more and more been identified in the popular mind as being 'the capital of Europe', and this process has had its own momentum despite its official designation as *provisoire*.

However, while the Belgian capital does possess great advantages it does not therefore follow that Parliament must also be located in it. There are examples of the democratic separation of powers being given expression in physical separation also[7]. It has been argued that the physical separation of the various agencies of Community government could be an acceptable alternative to their concentration in the traditional manner in one place. It has been proposed that a better long-term solution would be a division of functions, with, say, Brussels being the seat of the Council and Commission, Luxembourg of Parliament and Court and Strasbourg of the Council of Europe and its agencies. Psychologically, this could be an advantage, since it would give the institutions and their functions a greater definiteness in the minds of the Community's quarter of a billion inhabitants. The whole could well be obscured in the mélange of one great centralized 'Eurocapital', towards which hostility could easily be engendered[8]. It has also been argued that the current problems of the great European conurbations should give pause in the creation of what could develop into a 'Eurometropolis'. The dispersal of Community functions and activities over a wider area would be more in line with moves to stimulate activity in the regions and to lessen the grip of the centre. It could also be said to fit in better with the heterogeneous and polycentric nature of Europe, and thus possibly have a better chance of success in capturing the imagination of Europeans. This varied Europe already manifests itself in Florence, with its European University Institute, in Bruges, with the College of Europe and in Geneva and Vienna, with their wide range of European as well as international organizations.

In support of this devolutionary line of thought there is also the fact that technological revolution has now begun to make concentration in one place less obligatory than it might have been in the past. The first international city of modern times was Geneva, headquarters of the League of Nations. Although it had all the right international credentials, it soon came to be realized that the maintenance of speedy communications with the national capitals was a major problem. Its relative isolation on the edge of the Alps undoubtedly contributed to the problems which the League was unable to handle. Now, after more than half a century, the continent is bound together with a comprehensive air network and is meshed with international telephones and teleprinters. Information can be flashed virtually instantaneously across the continent, and diplomats at international gatherings can be almost continuously in touch with their governments. These developments have made the dispersal of international functions now a practical possibility, and such dispersal could possess physical and psychological advantages for the Community's successful development.

Another idea put forward has been that of a purpose-built European capital city located in a federal territory on the model of Washington, Brasilia and many other such places. Marshall Miller's main reason for arguing the merits of this is that no existing city is adequate for this function, and there is need of a focal point for the movement towards European unity[9]. His proposed location of this 'Lake Europa' was at the junction of the frontiers of Luxembourg, France and West Germany. This would actually put it a mere 20 km south-east of Luxembourg, the implication of this being that, of the existing cities, Luxembourg has the most satisfactory location. This and other similar ideas have, however, never been followed up. This is partly a matter of the enormous cost of such a project and also partly because of the fact that such capitals have not been spectacularly successful in recent times. The grafting of 'Eurocapital' functions onto an existing large city has been considered to be a more satisfactory process.

The European Communities between them employ directly and indirectly some 16 000 people, three-quarters of whom work in the three 'Eurocities' alone. Brussels, with nearly a half of all those in Community employment, stands head and shoulders above the others (*Figure 6.2*). Luxembourg comes second, but Strasbourg has only a small number of Community employees, although it is the workplace of most of those in the service of the Council of Europe[10]. In addition to those employed by the four large Community institutions, there are a number of other organiza-

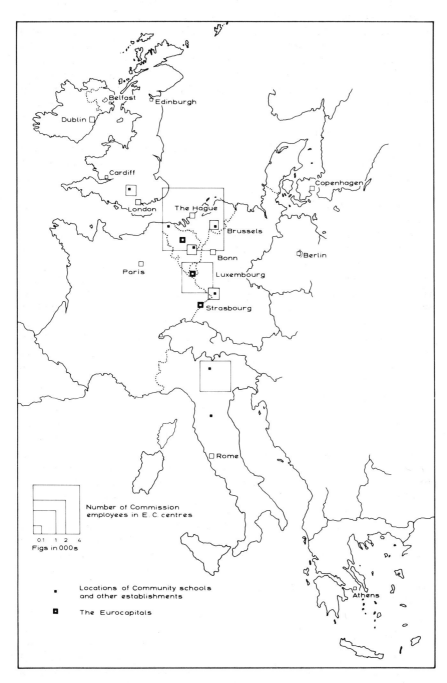

Figure 6.2 The distribution of Community activities

tions within the Community orbit mainly engaged in research, education and information. The most important of these are the five establishments coming under the umbrella of the Joint Research Centre[11], the eight European Schools and the EC offices located in each of the Community's capital cities and a number overseas. There are also the European University Institute, established in Florence in 1975, and the College of Europe at Bruges, which dates from 1950. Throughout the Community's territory there are twenty-one locations in which Community and associated international activity is taking place. They are to be found in each of the ten member states, but their centre of gravity is the delta-Rhineland core, within which no fewer than eleven of them are located and which accounts for nine-tenths of all employees. It is thus in the Community's germinal region itself that its activity still appears to be most in evidence. It is here that the existence of the Community is most tangible, and its physical presence reinforces the many other transnational features already identified in this region.

Thus we have a situation where the whole of this central region, most advantageously located in relation to the Community as a whole and with an international cultural and economic infrastructure more highly developed than elsewhere, is essentially the physical centre of gravity of Community activity also. As has been seen, the new Europe is being created around the great cultural and political divide of the past. The formidable frontier fortresses have been transformed within decades into executive and administrative centres. Mackinder talked of the 'great capital of the Rhinelands'[12], which consisted of a group of competing cities. Perhaps the logic of the present situation is that the 'Eurocities', and possibly others as well, should now be regarded as Europe's collective capital, collaborating rather than competing, linked together more effectively by the means of communication which are now technically possible. Allied to this there is also the aim of encouraging a spread of European activities into the more far-flung parts of the continent.

Notes

1. France withdrew from the NATO Command Structure in 1966 in conformity with General de Gaulle's desire to promote an independent French foreign policy. The NATO headquarters, which had been located in Paris since 1949, was then instructed to leave the city
2. The population of Brussels is 1 million, Luxembourg 77 000 and Strasbourg 257 000
3. 'Is the Council aware that for the Parliament to have three places of work is costing the taxpayer £16 million a year and is resulting in the staff being inefficient and overworked?' asked Alan Tyrrell (UK, ED). In reply, Giuseppe Zamberletti said a decision on the seat was a political matter calling for unanimity on the part of member governments. Until they reached agreement no change would be possible. Proceedings of the European Parliament, 12 March, 1980
4. The new *Palais de l'Europe* was completed in 1978. It was then the only building really capable of accommodating the 410 members of the Parliament which was directly elected in 1979. Like its predecessor, the *Maison de l'Europe*, it belongs to the Council of Europe and is rented by the Communities
5. 'The capital city reflects the wealth, power and political organization of the state of which it is the administrative centre . . . [Capital cities] incarnate the corelands that have evolved as nationalities'. (Whittlesey, *The Earth and the State*)

6. Geneva, headquarters of the League of Nations, had been Europe's first international city of modern times. It possessed the impeccable internationalist credentials of centrality, democracy and neutrality. It was idyllically situated in the Swiss mountains, but this was also the basis of its great disadvantage. Communications with governments were slow, and this held up international action by the League
7. A European instance of this is the Netherlands, where the functions of central government are divided between The Hague and Amsterdam
8. Responsibility for problems and discontents associated with the capital and the government are tending now to be transferred, with government connivance, to Brussels. This is already seen as the home of the 'faceless bureaucrats', allegedly running the continent insensitively from behind their desks
9. J. M. Miller, *Lake Europa: A New Capital for a United Europe*, New York, 1963
10. The Council of Europe has some 500 full-time employees
11. The Joint Research Centre is the collective name for the EC's four nuclear research establishments together with the Joint European Torus. The research establishments are located at Ispra (Italy), Karlsruhe (German Federal Republic), Geel (Belgium) and Petten (Netherlands). The JET was established in 1979 at Culham (England)
12. Mackinder, 'Geographical Conditions affecting the British Empire'

Chapter 7

Community Europe as a potential superpower

Underlying the urgent problems with which Europe was faced in the early 1950s, and for which the Community was seen as a solution, there was also the inherent attractiveness of the idea of European unity. This had many causes, but one of them was certainly the restoration by collective action of some of the world power and influence which Europe had lost after World War II. The Eurocentric world system was by this time a mere shadow of what it had been even a quarter of a century earlier, and the reality was that the continent was effectively imprisoned within the neo-imperial structures of the new world giants. A powerful strand in European thinking at the time was concerned with the reassertion of independence and the resumption of control over its own destiny. From the east there was the perceived danger emanating from the Soviet Union, now firmly in control of a wide European buffer zone, and seemingly poised to resolve the German question, by force if necessary. From the West there came the more subtle, but nonetheless real, danger of absorption into the American dollar-based economic empire which was spreading its tentacles throughout the Western world. The idea implicit in the saying that 'Russia wants to conquer Europe but America wants to buy her' contained some very unpalatable truths about the new relationship between the two sides of the Atlantic. The colony had become the colonizer, and the imperial periphery had come to dominate the old centre.

The individual European states, and even the erstwhile great powers, were on their own much too small and weak to rival either superpower, and clearly a more independent position could only be achieved through a measure of cooperation. As the former French Prime Minister, Paul Reynaud, put it in 1950, 'Everyone believes that between the two giants there is a place for Europe, but not for the patchwork of European states'[1]. Another French Prime Minister, Maurice Faure, speaking to the National Assembly in 1957 stated the geopolitical position with admirable clarity:

We are living again today on a fiction which consists of saying that there are four great powers in the world. This is not true. There are not four great powers but only two: America and Russia. There will be a third at the end of the century: China. It depends on you whether there will be a fourth: Europe.[2]

Thus one of the elements in the composite movement towards European unity was the existence of a sort of fifth column for the liberation of Europe, which could lead in turn in the direction of an international 'third force'. The end-product of this line of thinking, whether its protagonists welcomed it or not, was the creation of a sort of European superpower. In order to determine how realistic this idea is it is necessary to examine the geopolitical features of the two existing superpowers, and to evaluate the foundations upon which their great strength rests.

The United States and the Soviet Union did not suddenly emerge in the middle of the twentieth century like genii out of an international bottle. They had both been among the nine acknowledged 'powers' fifty years earlier, but they had both been peripheral to the largely Eurocentric world order of the time[3]. World War I demonstrated both the immense strength of the United States and the fact that Russia had become a 'paper tiger'. After this war was over both retreated into some isolation from the mainstream of world affairs, the new Soviet Union to build up her strength under the Communist régime, and America to enjoy her immense wealth unencumbered by foreign entanglements. By adopting these attitudes, they permitted the Eurocentric world order to continue for one last generation. After this they were both forced to re-enter world affairs by being themselves attacked[4], and they then combined together with Britain to form the victorious Grand Alliance. Less than a decade later they were bestriding the world like twin colossi, each having a large sphere of influence beyond its own frontiers.

The explanation of the paramountcy of these two out of the nine great powers at the turn of the century can be traced to their geopolitical characteristics. They are both very large countries, the United States with over 9 million km^2 and the Soviet Union over 22 million km^2. This makes them respectively 17 times and 40 times the size of France, the largest Community state. Each consists of massive compact blocks of territory in which the ratio of frontier to total area is low. East-to-west extent in both cases is considerably in excess of that from north to south, and this has resulted in relatively homogeneous physical conditions throughout large parts of their territories. They centre on the great mid-latitude belts which possess similar overall climatic, vegetational and soil conditions. The United States, however, as a result of its more southerly location has in general warmer and more potentially productive conditions.

Both countries also have very large populations, many times more than even the biggest European states. The Soviet Union has four times, and the United States over three times the population of the German Federal Republic, the Community's most populous state. However, demographic size is in neither case anything like as great as is territorial extent, and consequently overall densities of population are very low by European standards (*Table 7.1*). No member of the EC(10) has a population density anything like as low as the United States' 23 per km^2 and the Soviet Union's 12 per km^2. Concentrations are greatest in the respective core regions of the central part of European Russia and the north-eastern quadrilateral of the United States, where densities actually approach European levels (*Figure 7.1*). Both of these cores are surrounded by areas of very moderate density and beyond them are huge, relatively empty

TABLE 7.1. Comparative statistics for the extent, population and production of the European Communities, the United States and the Soviet Union

	EC(10)	USA	USSR
Area (million km^2)	1.66	9.4	22.4
Population (million)	269.9	220.6	264.1
Density (per km^2)	163	24	12
Primary energy production (toe)	455.3	1485	1327
Primary energy consumption (toe)	985.1	1816	N.A.
Petroleum production (million tonnes)	89.0	488	602
Iron ore (million tonnes)	38.8	86.5	246
Crude steel (million tonnes)	140.2	126.1	149
Shipbuilding (million tonnes)	2.4	0.8	N.A.
Motor vehicles (million)	12.0	11.5	2.2
Gross Domestic Product (mrd EUA)	1960	1886	N.A.

Source: EC Statistical Office, Luxembourg, 1981

territories. These were the 'frontiers' of settlement, and they still have very different and usually less stable cultural features than those characteristic of either the Russian or the American heartland. They remain sparsely settled, and to a large extent are engaged in primary production of various sorts.

Within their vast territories both powers have a great variety of physical resources, biological and geological, and this is reflected in their output of energy, metals, fibres, wood, chemicals and foodstuffs. Collectively, they are the world's two largest producers of a whole range of natural resources, and this has given them a considerable measure of self-sufficiency and independence. Both are also the major producers of a wide range of industrial goods including iron and steel, non-ferrous metals, heavy engineering products, textiles and chemicals, and indigenously produced raw materials supply the greater part of the requirements of these industries. The high degree of independence of both countries is also seen in their relatively small shares of international trade in relation to GDPs. The imports of the United States make up only just over 6 per cent of her total GDP and this contrasts markedly with the United Kingdom's 23 per cent and the Netherlands' massive 43 per cent. The GDP of the United States in 1981 was 1886 million ECU – over three times that of the German Federal Republic, the Community's largest economy. While the GDP of the Soviet Union is not calculated in Western terms, estimates suggest that

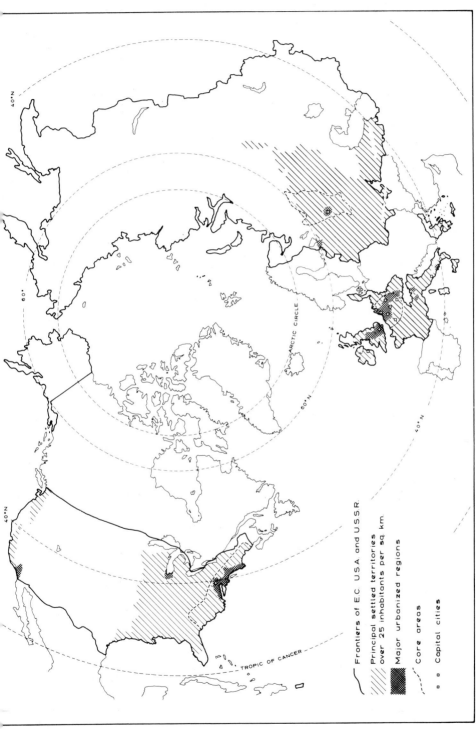

Figure 7.1 Community Europe and the superpowers

it is around 40 per cent of that of the United States. In spite of this considerable economic discrepancy between the two superpowers, the economy of the Soviet Union is still far larger than that of any third country.

Another characteristic which they have in common is the large measure of heterogeneity in their populations. This has arisen from the fact that they are in different ways both 'imperial' in demographic composition. The Soviet Union is quite clearly an empire built up over the centuries through the expansion of the Russians into the territories of other Slav and Asiatic peoples. The United States was initially an anti-imperial state, populated by those who went there in search of freedom and material prosperity. This was the 'life, liberty and the pursuit of happiness' enshrined in the American constitution and part of the American dream. In the Soviet Union the Russians are the dominant nationality, the most patriotic, Communist and prominent in the high positions in the land. In America this position has been held by those of British descent and culture. More specifically, it is the White Anglo-Saxon Protestants – WASPS – who have been the dominant group and the custodians of established social values. Expressed in geopolitical terms, these hegemonies have been exercised from the heartlands of central Russia and the north-east seaboard of the United States. They are the two regions from which the power of the respective countries emerged during the seventeenth and eighteenth centuries, and from which it has ever since been wielded. While in the Soviet Union this power is officially vested in the proletariat and justified by the doctrine of Marxism, the reality is that it has been highly statist and in the Muscovite tradition of centralization. In the United States also power is deemed to emanate from the people, but in practice for most of the time it has been exercised by an east coast elite promoting WASP values with the consent of the governed. In both cases, now, a geographic-al, economic and cultural pre-eminence has been translated into the possession and wielding of considerable power in the name of specified ideals. These ideals actually derive from the sublimation of particular responses to indigenous conditions; they were very much a product of the soil which has given rise to them and in which they have flourished. The particular features of the power base are the possession of considerable physical resources, industrial strength and a strong will to translate these things into military power. Since World War II this has in both cases been exercised messianically in the name of a system of ideas, an ideology, which is claimed to have global applicability.

A number of these superpower characterisics can be identified in the European Community, but size is certainly not one of them. The total area of EC(10) is 1½ million km², and this is only one-sixth that of the United States and one-fifteenth that of the Soviet Union (*Figure 7.1*). Neither does it have that compactness of form possessed by the two superpowers. It has very long frontiers and coastlines in relation to its total area. Nearly half of the total area is either insular or peninsular in relation to the central mass of the quadrilateral and northern Italy. While, as has been observed, the two superpowers have a far greater east-to-west than north-to-south extent, the situation of the Community is quite the opposite (*Figure 7.1*). It extends over 25 degrees of latitude while the United States covers only 23 degrees but the United States has a substantially greater east-to-west extent, while the Soviet Union's is over four times as much. This results in the Community having considerable north–south physical diversity but a much smaller proportion of mid-latitude physical homogeneity. Thus, in basic physical characteristics, there appears to be very little resemblance between the Community and the superpowers.

Turning now to human geography, the Community's total population of 270 million is of the same order as those of both superpowers, being slightly greater than that of the Soviet Union. In view of its far smaller area this results in an overall population density of 170 per km^2, seven times that of the United States and sixteen times that of the Soviet Union. Only in the core regions of the two superpowers do population densities reach anything like this level. The resource situation in the Community is also very different. The industrial growth of the countries of Western Europe in the last century had been founded on the great wealth of coal, iron, non-ferrous metals, textile fibres and foodstuffs, the latter to feed the growing proletariats. By the beginning of the present century the position was in process of rapid change, and the industrialized countries were becoming increasingly dependent on imports for most of their foodstuffs and primary raw materials. This dependence continued to increase, so that by 1970 nearly two-thirds of all the resource requirements of the countries of EC(10) had to be imported from third countries. Significant among these were energy, metals, textile fibres, tropical produce, wood and foodstuffs. The high levels of self-sufficiency in primary materials which have characterized the two superpowers are thus not at all characteristic of the Community.

In the matter of overall industrial strength, the Community's situation is again a different one. The combined GDP of the EC(10) is now virtually the same as that of the United States, and consequently considerably in excess of that of the Soviet Union. General industrial output, excepting only energy and metallurgy, compares favourably with them both. In the production of motor vehicles, shipbuilding, chemicals, plastics and man-made fibres the Community is in the same class as the United States, and therefore considerably stronger than the Soviet Union.

It has been seen that both superpowers have unitary core regions which are their principal centres of gravity in political, economic, demographic and cultural terms. At the other extreme territorially are the huge empty hinterlands from which are drawn the supplies of physical resources to supply the requirements of these cores and the other main centres of population and industry. As has been seen, a core–periphery structure on a continental scale has been identified in the European Community but this is not comparable with the structures of the two superpowers. Europe's continental core is more the result of a running together of national cores, and, although it possesses a degree of economic and demographic pre-eminence, it does not as yet possess the political and wider cultural ascendancy which could translate this strength into power. This still remains with the member states, and it has been used most effectively by France and Germany in steering the Community in directions most congenial to them. Neither is there a hinterland in any way comparable with those of the superpowers, and so there is no 'frontier' from which raw materials can readily be obtained. The Community's territory is for the most part densely populated, the only relatively lightly populated areas being around the western and southern fringes. By superpower standards the Community is almost all industrial core and no primary-producing periphery, the latter having until recently been the colonial empires from which much of the requirements of primary produce was obtained.

It follows from this that there is no real dominant region in the Community and no dominant national/cultural group of the WASP type. Instead there is a collection of national languages and cultures, many of them more closely related to languages and cultures outside the Community than to those within it. This is one of the principal legacies of the oceanic and expansionist phase in European history. It is a situation which has contributed to the deep divisions over the question of the Community's *lingua franca*, the principal contenders being the major ex-imperial, and now neo-imperial, languages – French and English. Yet beneath these very real divisions lie the unifying ideals which the Community was established to propagate. These relate particularly to individual liberty, democracy and a pluralist system, and they have been a powerful cement in binding together countries which in other ways remain so diverse.

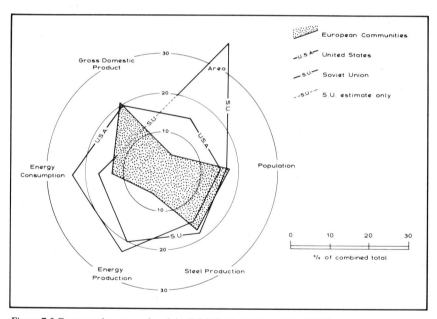

Figure 7.2 Comparative strengths of the EC(10), the USA and the USSR

From all this it appears that there is a close correspondence between the Community and the two superpowers only in the attributes of total population and overall economic strength. In all the others – size and shape, physical resources, internal spatial structure, homogeneity and the degree of unity – there are considerable differences. In these attributes the Community is just not in the same league. However, changes which have been in process in recent decades are tending to alter the situation.

One of these changes has resulted from the increased Community interest in achieving greater self-sufficiency in physical resources. Dependence on imports had steadily increased since the end of the nineteenth century under the pressure from rapid industrialization, increased home production costs and the relative ease with which cheaper raw materials could be imported from dependent territories and elsewhere. However, by the end of the 1960s the world had become a far less comfortable place for the countries of Western Europe to live in, and greater self-sufficiency began to be a more attractive option. Throughout the present century the continent had come to be regarded as being increasingly 'run down' in natural resources, but from the 1960s onwards important new discoveries were to be made. Dependence on imports had become most critical in the energy field, and especially in the supply of oil, which accounted for over a half of all the energy consumed in EC(10). By 1972 98 per cent of the oil consumed in the EC(10) was imported, and there was dependence on imports for 64 per cent of the total energy requirement. This was an acceptable, even welcome, situation when oil was both cheap and plentiful, but the oil crisis of 1973 changed this situation totally. Following the massive increases in the price of crude by the Organization of Petroleum Exporting Countries (OPEC) and the new strength and unity of the producers in relation to the consumers, the scale of the dependence was now seen to be highly dangerous both economically and politically. In tackling the problem the Community was aided first by the discovery and exploitation of large reserves of natural gas in the Netherlands and the southern part of the North Sea, followed by huge oil reserves further north in the North Sea. There was also an increased interest in the coal industry, the output of which had been declining since the 1950s in the face of competition from imported coal and oil. Resources nevertheless remained considerable, especially in Britain and West Germany, and rich new seams were brought into production. Nuclear energy also began to make a more substantial contribution, and between 1970 and 1980 it increased from 4.5 to 11 per cent of the Community's net electricity output. As a result of all these developments, dependence on energy imports was reduced from 64 per cent of consumption in 1972 to 54 per cent in 1980, in spite of an increased energy consumption of 70 million tonnes oe in EC(10) over this period. With increasing energy production from the North Sea and emphasis on the development of other types of indigenous energy, together with the implementation by the Community of measures for energy conservation, it appears that the degree of dependence on imports is likely to continue to decrease.

Another important area of increased self-sufficiency is in food supply. The Community is now able to produce the greater part of its requirement of temperate foodstuffs; a greatly changed situation from that of the earlier part of the century. Europe's agriculture did not keep up with the industrialization and, as a consequence, an increased dependence on imports was considered to be quite normal. The most extreme example of this was Britain, which in the 1930s imported some two-thirds of its food requirements. Since the 1950s considerable modernization has been occurring, and the effects of this have been particularly dramatic in countries such as France and Italy, in which agriculture had been most backward.

The key to this development has been technical improvement and greater agricultural specialization throughout Europe. An unfortunate accompaniment of this process has been the production of large food surpluses, which have frequently formed 'mountains' and 'lakes' because of the difficulty of disposal at the high prices which are features of the Common Agricultural Policy.

Finally, the rise in world commodity prices has frequently resulted in supply problems, so increasing the incentive to exploit other indigenous resources. These include non-ferrous metals, timber, chemicals and textile fibres which have been making an increased, although usually limited, contribution.

It has been seen that the levels of political and cultural homogeneity, and of establishment consensus, in the decision-making centres are low in the Community by comparison with the superpowers. This is no more than might be expected at this stage, since the Community is, after all, an attempt to fuse the previous generation of world powers which had, over the centuries, developed their own internal political/cultural systems and had reinforced them through mutual antagonism. The successful superimposition of a new unitary structure on these could be expected to take time. Many changes have taken place, important amongst which are those stemming from the high levels of intra-Community transactions together with the particular tendency to homogenization in the central areas, the European 'melting pot'. This has been accompanied by an increasing tendency to 'convergence' in policies by the member countries, so making possible a consensus for the development of new inititiatives along the lines of the successful Common Agricultural Policy[5]. Tentative, if often faltering and inadequate, steps have also been taken in the fields of regional development[6], aids to industry, energy conservation, transport coordination and environmental protection which are based upon the premise that there are shared interests which can most effectively be tackled jointly. 'Convergence' can also be found in the area of foreign policy with the beginnings of the formation of a concerted 'European view' on such issues as the Middle East, Latin America and the Communist countries[7]. This is, of course, well founded in the strand of European thinking which seeks to consolidate the independence of Europe in strength through unity.

The Community has its emerging core–periphery structure, but it does not possess those empty hinterlands which played such an important role in the development of both the United States and the Soviet Union. As has been observed, this was a role formerly played for the European countries by their empires which, with their 'blood and sand', 'thin red lines' and colourful savages, became the exciting and romantic frontiers of their cultures[8]. Shorn of the imperial possessions, Europe now became in effect an ecumene without a hinterland. This was in many ways as much of a psychological as a physical problem, since the alleged need for *lebenstraum* can be very much a state of mind. Post-imperial – or, in some minds neo-colonial – thinking has led to suggestions for the development of close new ties. One such geopolitical concept is that of 'Eurafrica', a sort of pan-region which could operate to the mutual benefit of both continents, the one highly industrialized and the other rich in physical resources. Close economic associations with the former dependent territories, especially those in Africa, have been developed, and they constitute an important part of the Community's external relations (*see* Chapter 8). Cohen proposed a 'Europe-Maghreb' geopolitical region with a frontier of development south into the Sahara[9]. This area produces oil, natural gas and metals, and has considerable potential for sub-tropical agriculture. Such a Community frontier south of the Mediterranean and extending deep into the Sahara would in many ways resemble the hinterlands of the superpowers. Indeed Mussolini's *mare nostrum* of the 1930s and the *Algérie française* in the 1950s were both attempts to establish the ascendancy of Europe in just such a way as this. The Mediterranean is now identified as one of the Community's hardest frontiers. It appears highly unlikely at the moment that movement will take place into an area which is so politically, historically and culturally different, is at a much lower level of economic development and, perhaps above all, retains a vestigial suspicion towards the former European imperial powers.

The other Community 'frontier' is to the north, where the Arctic and sub-Arctic islands appear to have considerable potential in resources. They all have historic associations with Scandinavia, and are as near as the Scandinavians got to the establishment of empires. The Faroe Islands are a Danish dependency, and Greenland, a former dependency, became in 1980 a self-governing part of the Danish Kingdom[10]; Spitzbergen is Norwegian and Iceland is an independent state within the Western orbit and a member of NATO. They are all very lightly populated, especially so Greenland, which has a total population less than that of the city of Luxembourg on an area as large as the whole of the EC(10)[11]. It is believed to possess considerable mineral wealth, but is still largely unsurveyed, the greater part of it being covered by an enormous ice sheet. Currently of far greater importance are the resources of the continental shelf, and especially the North Sea. The total area of this is as large as those of France and West Germany combined, and it is now the major indigenous producer of natural gas, petroleum and fish. This, together with the rest of the continental shelf swathing the north and west of the Community, already constitutes a resource frontier. It may prove also to have similar psychological ingredients to those possessed by the former imperial possessions. It is large, rich and empty, and new technologies with a Jules Verne flavour could make it into the 'maritime frontier' of the future.

Geopolitical shifts and adjustments are the spatial manifestations of the search for better relationships between the various elements which go to make up societies. The aim is in the direction of producing units of organization which are best adapted to cater culturally, economically and politically for the well-being of their peoples. It was the inadequacies within the industrial societies of Western Europe which ultimately gave birth to their maritime empires. As a result of the stresses within these, caused by the different aspirations of the subject-peoples, it proved impossible to maintain them after the middle years of the twentieth century. Denuded of these powerful economic, demographic and psychological props, the West European countries were forced at the time to make a radical reappraisal of their positions in the world. The end-product of this was that, for the majority of them, imperial ideas were gradually discarded in favour of continental ones, and climbing the Alps and crossing the Rhine and, eventually, crossing the Channel were seen to be the creative and positive responses to the new situation in which they found themselves. If we take into account the changes which have been outlined, then the unit which emerged out of this has now many characteristics of a superpower. What appears to be still in short supply, in comparison with the existing superpowers, are collective will and physical resources, although these factors also are in course of change. There certainly appears to be potentially the kind of muscle which could enable the Community to take its place as Maurice Faure's 'quatrième grand' by the end of the century.

Over the period of the development of the Community the superpowers themselves have not been totally unchanging. They may have reached a kind of plateau of joint world power and influence, but internal changes have been subtly altering their world roles. The high level of resource self-sufficiency has been tending to diminish, a situation which is the result both of depletion and of increases in internal demand. This is a similar development to that which began in Western Europe during the last century. It is especially a problem of the economic core regions, which have for long now had to rely on the resources of their hinterlands in order to redress the imbalance. The involvement of the powers with the rest of the world, which they both undertook in the late 1940s with military and strategic considerations in mind, has now become essential to their economic well-being. The Soviet Union remains well behind the United States in terms of economic strength and technological innovation, and the relative positions of the two do not appear to have substantially altered in recent times. In spite of its tremendous physical resources and impressive industrial base, the Soviet Union is dependent on the West for imports of food and advanced technology. The real explanation of the Soviet Union's impressive power is to be found less in her sheer size and resources than in the centralized control by the state. It is this which permits the continued existence of very high levels of military expenditure in relation to total GDP. The development of American military might is also closely related to the advances of 'big government' both in and after World War II. As a result of her far greater wealth, she was able to accomplish this with the expenditure of far less effort.

The European Community as yet lacks the political and cultural homogeneity or establishment consensus to transform its economic strength into political and military power. EDC, WEU, NATO's Euro-group and the meetings of foreign ministers have represented attempts to move in this direction, but none have been backed by the necessary political will to transform them into something more concrete. Consequently, in spite of a GDP as large as that of the United States, the EC(10) is still ultimately dependent upon the transatlantic connection for its defence. In Cohen's world concept, the EC, together with the rest of maritime Europe, constitutes a geopolitical region embedded in a geo-strategic one, the latter being the Atlantic Alliance as a whole. Looked at in this light, it is what Laqueur has referred to as a 'civilian power'[12]. While it has successfully achieved a 'Pax Bruxellana' in Western Europe, it neither has, nor at the moment aspires to, the independent military power with which to pursue its goals in the world.

Notes

1. Paul Reynaud, to the French National Assembly in 1950
2. Maurice Faure, in a speech to the National Assembly during the debate on French membership of the European Economic Community in 1957
3. These were the United Kingdom, France, Germany, Austria–Hungary, Russia, Italy, the Ottoman Empire, the United States and Japan. The process of elimination began with the collapse of the Ottoman and Austro–Hungarian Empires in 1918. With the defeat of Germany, Italy and Japan in 1945, together with the weak condition of France, this left the 'Big Three' of World War II, later to become the 'Big Four' of the post-war years. (*See also* Chapter 1, note 1)
4. The Soviet Union was invaded by Germany on 22 June 1941, and the American naval base at Pearl Harbour, Hawaii, was attacked by the Japanese on 7 December of the same year. This was, in Roosevelt's words, 'a day which will live in infamy', but it was to result in the United States, within five years, becoming overwhelmingly the most powerful country in the world
5. The Common Agricultural Policy has been successful in closely coordinating under supranational control responsibility for a particular sector. It does not automatically follow that this is a good or desirable policy in so far as its aims are concerned
6. There are many agencies engaged in regional matters and almost all Community economic intervention has a regional dimension to it. As Robert Marjolin, former Vice-President of the Commission, said, there are 'as many regional problems as there are regions'. The main thrust in the Community's development policy has been provided by the European Regional Development Fund (ERDF), established in 1976. Initially it was given a three-year budget of ECU 1300 millions and for the next three-year period this was raised to ECU 2090 millions. However, these sums were nothing like as much as had originally been asked for by the Commission and pressed for by Parliament. The ERDF repesents a very half-hearted approach to the whole regional question. The success of the Common Agricultural Policy in establishing its prior claim to funds has been an important factor in restricting the capacity of the Community to make available adequate funding in other areas of action
7. Meetings of the Foreign Ministers in Political Cooperation. This was established for the discussion of matters outside the strict terms of reference of the Treaties. As a result of these meetings, common positions have been reached on a variety of international questions
8. The conquest of the 'West' has become a national mythology which underpins the American self-image to this very day. The same psychology is to be found in *Beau Geste* and in films such as the immortal *Sanders of the River* (directed by Alexander Korda, 1935). As S. B. Cohen put it, 'These vast tracts of territory situated outside the ecumene are national morale boosters; their environment provides continuous challenge to the national spirit and genius'. (S. B. Cohen, *Geography and Politics in a World Divided*, 2nd edn, Oxford, 1973)
9. Ibid., Chapter 5
10. Following the achievement of sovereignty in internal matters in 1979, it became the proclaimed policy of the Greenland government to take the country out of the Community. The advisory referendum of February 1982 produced a small majority of 52 per cent in favour of withdrawal, while 46 per cent were against. It is the intention of the anti-EC Siumut government to withdraw from full membership, but to negotiate economic arrangements with the Community
11. The area of Greenland is 2 175 000 km^2. Its population in 1981 was 51 000
12. Walter Laqueur, *A Continent Astray*, Oxford, 1979

Chapter 8

Community Europe and the world

The countries of the European Community, and more particularly those of its maritime fringes, have for many centuries been intimately involved with the affairs of the rest of the world. By the beginning of the present century one of them at least had become more concerned with events in Africa or the antipodes than with those taking place in the Balkans or on the Rhine. The facts of geography were subjected to topological distortion to such an extent that the far-away countries were a matter of hundreds of miles away in central or eastern Europe, rather than thousands of miles away in other continents[1]. The winding down of these extra-European involvements was a major underlying factor in the new positive interest of the western European countries in Europe itself. This inevitably produced the diatribe that the Community was 'inward-looking' in its attitudes, and clearly this must have been true, since its very existence was, in part at least, a reaction to the approaching end of the 'outward-looking' phase in the history of maritime Europe. However, the web of global relationships, entering into almost every sphere of human activity, could hardly terminate abruptly with the end of the maritime empires themselves. The whole process entailed the reformulation of the relationships of the member countries not just with one another but with the world at large.

In order to understand the nature of the new relationships it is necessary to examime them against the background of the world scene which emerged around the middle of the present century. Until then it had, of course, been dominated, although with increasing difficulty, by the Eurocentric political and economic systems. After World War II these were rapidly replaced by the quasi-imperial systems of the two superpowers confronting each other antagonistically across the ruins of Europe. Since then forms of devolutionary power-sharing have been introduced into the spheres of influence of both. The American sphere has become the Atlantocentric Western alliance and the Soviet sphere is the Eastern bloc, centring on the Warsaw Pact. New centres of power, the European Community and China, have been born within each of these. Both of them emerged from a desire for regional autonomy in decision-making independent of either of the superpowers, but there are a number of important differences between them. The first is that the European Community, although economically far more advanced than China, lacks the latter's internal homogeneity which has resulted from millennia of unity. Britain and France, the last two vestigial global powers in Europe, have continued to maintain their own formidable power bases, extra-regional associations and nuclear weapons. Both have retained an independence of outlook which considerably inhibits the formulation of a united Community *weltanschaung*. The second major difference is that the Community has remained an integral part of a wider geostrategic system; transatlantic disagreements have been in a very low key when compared with the deterioration in Sino–Soviet relations in the 1960s. The Atlantic may have grown wider, but the Euro–American umbilical cord remained intact, while the 3000 km Sino–Soviet frontier became a hard shell separating increasingly antagonistic systems.

It is possible to construct a basic model of the world scene to illustrate the position of the Community. In it after World War II the world is divided into three macro-geopolitical regions: the West, the East and the South (or Third World) (*Figure 8.1*). From the 1950s onwards important new poles of power begin to emerge within each region, these being the European Community, China and the Arab countries. China moved out of the Soviet orbit, while the Community remained within the Western one, and the power of the Arabs is attributable to the concerted use of the 'oil weapon' through OPEC. In order to understand more precisely the Community's relationship to this tri-polar world order it is intended to adapt Churchill's idea of the 'three circles' of British interests in the 1940s[2] to an analogous 'three crescents' of European interests in the 1980s. These three crescents are maritime Europe, the West and the associated parts of the Third World, in particular Africa.

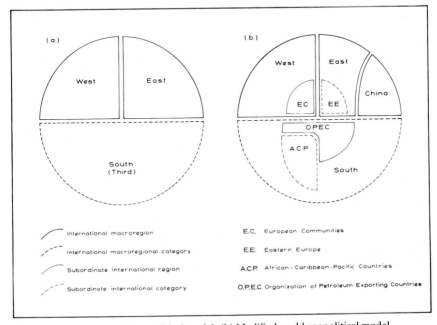

Figure 8.1 (a) Basic world geopolitical model; (b) Modified world geopolitical model

As a result of proximity, contiguity and economic and cultural overspill, it is with the adjacent countries of maritime Europe that relations are inevitably closest. Most of these countries are also institutionally connected through membership of NATO, OECD and the Council of Europe. To the north there is an overlap through the membership of Denmark with the Nordic Council and to the south in the eastern Mediterranean through Greece and Turkey, the latter having an association agreement with the EC. It has been seen that relationships in the areas of trade, investment, establishment, labour movement and cultural transactions are all at high levels. Contacts are closest of all with the countries of the Alps and Scandinavia, with which there are open frontiers and very high levels of international transaction. The transit traffic across the territories of Switzerland and Austria and the close connections between eastern Denmark and southern Sweden further add to the ease of transit across these frontiers. Membership of the Community by these countries would therefore appear to be a natural development, almost like an evolutionary process. That this has not happened, despite the coincidence of such an apparently favourable set of circumstances, can be attributed largely to factors operating within these countries themselves. They include the historic policies of neutrality pursued by both Sweden and Switzerland, the neutrality imposed on Austria by the peace treaty of 1955[3], and the narrow rejection of membership by the Norwegians in the 1972 referendum[4]. However, as members of EFTA these countries enjoy industrial free trade with the Community and they are for most purposes effectively client states within its economic orbit.

The second crescent of external interests is with the West as a whole and in particular with North America. Contacts have been institutionalized in NATO, OECD, GATT and, since 1975, through the 'economic summits' of the seven major Western powers[5]. Their combined domestic product makes up about two-thirds that of the West as a whole, and six of them are located around the shores of the North Atlantic Ocean. Transatlantic trade also accounts for some 15 per cent of the Community's total trade with third countries and North America is the source of almost all their investment and industrial establishment from external sources. Of greatest importance is the United States itself, which is the Community's largest single external trading partner and is of enormous economic significance in many other ways also. Through the North Atlantic umbilical a proliferation of technologies are transmitted, ranging from defence to fast foods. It is a flow which enters into most aspects of European life and indicates a major economic, technological and cultural diffusion from America to Europe. While in the 1950s American pre-eminence manifested itself mainly in the form of aid, it has now taken the form of various sorts of innovation or, as some might say, 'Americanization'. Politically, the Europeans and the Americans are now developing a 'special relationship' which in many ways replicates the features of the old Anglo-American 'special relationship' in the years after World War II[6].

A close relationship has also been in course of developing since the 1960s with Japan, that Western-style economic power in the Far East. Japan now supplies one-sixth of all the Community's imports of manufactures and an even larger proportion of motor vehicles and electrical and electronic

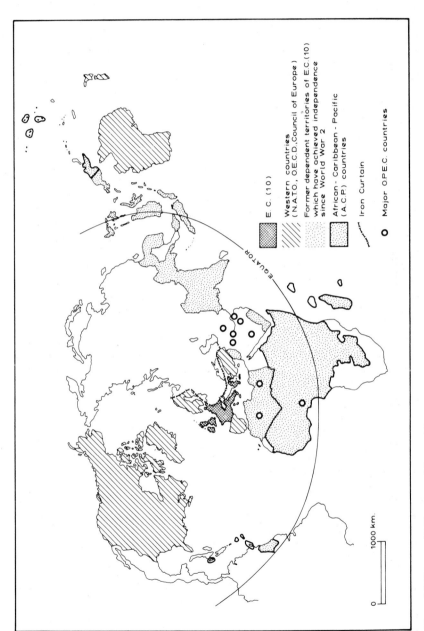

Figure 8.2 Community Europe and the world

equipment. The growing strength of this flow of imports has posed fundamental questions about the effectiveness of the Community's external trade policy.

The third crescent is in the South, the Third World of less developed countries, which in the past consisted mainly of the dependent territories of the European powers. At the time when the Treaty of Rome was signed some of the member states of the EC(6) still possessed substantial dependent territories, but most of these were to achieve their independence within the following five years. It was decided that after independence a new institutional relationship should be established with the Community as a whole, and this took the form of the Yaoundé Convention signed in 1963. It was the framework for a new economic relationship between the Community on the one hand, and the newly independent countries on the other. Its main provisions consisted of preferential trade agreements for a large group of products, together with a financial aid package from the Community to assist in economic development. This was additional to such aid as might continue to be given individually by the former colonial powers. This grouping of eighteen countries was known as the Association of African States and Madagascar[7] (AASM); in 1973 it became the AASMM with the adhesion of Mauritius. Following the enlargement of the Community in 1973 it was agreed that the whole arrangement should be reviewed and that the new provisions should also be applied to those ex-British dependent territories for which they were considered to be appropriate. The question of the relationship of the British Commonwealth as a whole to the European Community had been an issue since the first membership negotiations began in 1962, and it had proved to be a difficult one to resolve. The only Commonwealth members which could appropriately be included in an economic association of the Yaoundé type were those which were part of the less developed South, but there were not the resources available for all of these to be included. In 1975 the Yaoundé was replaced by the Lomé Convention, which initially had 46 signatories. By 1982 the number had already grown to 62.

These countries are collectively known as the African–Caribbean–Pacific (ACP) group and, although distributed widely across the world's poorest regions, there is a high concentration of them in Africa south of the Sahara (*Figure 8.2*). While they include some of the world's poorest and most backward countries, their collective strength is much boosted by the membership of the large ex-British colonies of Nigeria, Ghana, Kenya, Tanzania and Zimbabwe. The unitary character of the African ACP group is reinforced by geographical proximity, ethnic similarity, membership of the Organization for African Unity and broadly similar policies pursued in relation to Europe. There is, however, a major historical and linguistic divide, which dates from the colonial period between Francophone and Anglophone Africa, and this mirrors externally the similar divide which has been seen to exist within the Community itself.

The Lomé Convention has certain important features which makes it a step forward from Yaoundé. There is preferential access to the Community market for exports from the signatories, but reverse preferences are not obligatory so long as much-favoured-nation treatment is accorded. Revenues arising from exports of primary products are maintained by the

STABEX scheme for the adjustment of earnings over a period of time. The authority for the working of the Convention lies with the ACP–EC Council of Ministers, under the direction of which works a Committee of Ambassadors. There is also a Consultative Assembly which monitors the progress of the Convention, a committee to promote industrial coopera-tion and a Centre for Industrial Development located in Brussels.

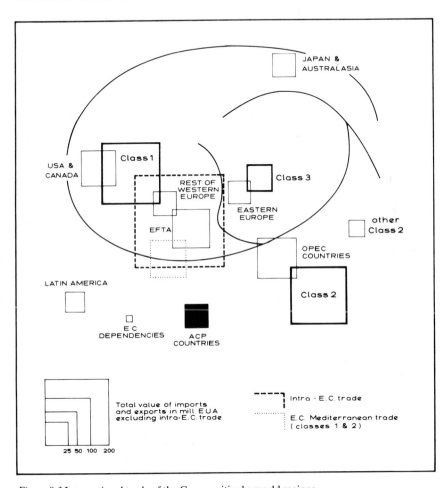

Figure 8.3 International trade of the Communities by world regions

The Lomé Convention is of considerable importance to the signatories since it secures them assured markets for their products at maintained prices and financial aid for their development. About a half of all ACP exports are to the Community, and the latter is the source of about the same proportion of their imports. The greater part of their exports consists of tropical plantation products, minerals and petroleum. Most of the latter comes from one country, Nigeria, which has in recent years become one of the world's largest producers. Basically, the trade pattern is in many ways a continuation of the economic relationship characteristic of the colonial period. However, while in the early part of the century western Europe's needs of primary products were drawn widely from all parts of the world, there has developed increasing concentration on Africa – a continent which was formerly of much less importance than Asia and the Americas. This relates to the closeness of the association with Africa which has been growing throughout the present century and of which the Lomé Convention is now but one manifestation. In spite of this, it does not, at the time being, appear to be the basis for any wider political or international grouping. Coming so close on the heels of the prolonged and often bloody struggles for independence from the Europeans, which was only attained by Zimbabwe as recently as 1980, any suggestion of 'neo-colonialism' is likely to prove to be extremely unpalatable.

In addition to the Community's own relationships with the former dependent territories, there are those directly between them and the ex-imperial powers themselves. The most important such persisting relationships are those between Britain and France and their former dependent territories, and these have been institutionalized in the British Commonwealth and the French Community, both of which have their own associative apparatus and their links at various levels. Most of these countries also come within the 'three crescent' system of Community external relationships. Outside them are the Commonwealth and ex-Commonwealth countries of southern and south-east Asia, in particular, those of the Indian subcontinent, whose neutralist stance has kept them out of firm international commitments. Yet the old relationship with Britain has not died, and the contacts continue in trade, investment, sport and cultural exchanges. In general they are now, however, at lower levels than those with the countries within the 'three crescents'.

The Community's relations with the Arab countries do not entirely fit either with the contemporary of the former links between Europe and the less developed world. Except for the southern shores of the Mediterranean, hardly any of the Arab lands came within the maritime European empires. For four hundred years they had been part of the Ottoman Empire and remained lightly populated, poor, remote and, for the most part, outside the main maritime European sphere of interest. What was to completely change the Western perception of them was the discovery in the early part of the present century that they possessed large reserves of oil, a commodity which was becoming of increasing importance following the invention of the internal combustion engine. As has been seen, in the years following World War II the countries of the Community became increasingly dependent on imported oil as it steadily replaced coal as their most important source of energy. In the late 1940s nine-tenths of all the Community's energy requirements were supplied from indigenous sources, while twenty-five years later the proportion had fallen to under two-fifths. This situation put the Community countries into a position of increasing vulnerability, and the danger signs of this were a number of oil supply crises, in particular the Suez Crisis of 1956[9]. The situation once more came to a head following the Israeli–Egyptian war of 1973[10], after which the Arabs invoked the 'oil weapon' to put pressure on the West. The new-found economic muscle was coordinated by OPEC, and by the early 1980s there had been a massive transfer of wealth from the Western

European oil-consuming countries to the mainly Arab oil producers. This was transformed into massive projects for economic development, aid to the rest of the Third World and a powerful build-up of armaments. Largely as a consequence of this upheaval, the Community experienced a recession from 1974 onwards which slowed down rates of growth and produced high levels of inflation. The Arab countries, and especially those around the Persian Gulf, now became more significant than ever to the Community. Out of this came the period of mutual consultations known as the 'Euro–Arab Dialogue' which took place over the period 1975 to 1979. It was an attempt to arrive at a new relationship between the two and to accommodate Arab interests in the new situation produced by increased Arab economic muscle as opposed to greater European weakness. It succeeded in establishing something of a *modus vivendi* between them, but it eventually foundered as a result of the reluctance of the Community to enter into a discussion of wider political as well as specifically economic issues. Although, as a result of the crisis, there was a tendency to convergence in the policies of the member countries in regard to the Arabs and the problems of the Middle East in general, there was neither the will nor the power to set about attempting to solve them. The lessons of 1956 had been learned, and active non-involvement became the European stance in the 1970s. There is also the realization that the strength of the Arabs is still narrowly based on the importance of a single vital commodity, and it will take a very long time before they can be in any sense really developed countries. The proportion of the Community's energy requirements deriving from imports has also been decreasing[11], and this naturally leads to further changes in the volatile Euro–Arab relationship.

It is a significant commentary on the external orientation of the Community that some of those countries which are in closest geographical proximity to it, sharing long land frontiers with overspilling physical and human features, are outside the 'three crescents'. With the Eastern European countries bound together in a geopolitical grouping around the Soviet Union, the Community's eastern frontier became the hardest dividing line of the Cold War, and the glacis of the Western alliance. It is even more significant, since it is one of the few places where the frontiers of the Community and those of the West as a whole coincide.

The rise of the Community as a potentially autonomous centre of power was inevitably disturbing to both superpowers. It was the place where confrontation between them had first developed after World War II, and it remained the most likely battlefield in any future war between them. The fact that the Atlantic Alliance was dominated by the overwhelming power of the Americans was a situation not totally displeasing to the Soviets, since it brought some order to the factious West and helped to control Germany[12]. At the same time, since the alliance was made up of fifteen sovereign states, the Soviets could attempt to further their own national interests by attempting to play them off one against the other. The major example of Western internecine feuding was in the strained relations between France and the Anglo-Saxon countries during the presidency of de Gaulle from 1958 to 1969. The French made difficult bedfellows in all the Western organizations: in 1965 they temporarily withdrew from the Community, leaving an 'empty chair'[13], and four years later they withdrew from the command structure of NATO, forcing the headquarters of the organization to leave Paris. In pursuance of a foreign policy of *stratégie tous azimuts*[14] the French entered at the same time into closer relations with the Soviet Union. Trade, technological exchanges and specialist visits were stepped up, and it looked for a time as though France, although under an authoritarian régime of the right, was paradoxically embarked on an international course which would eventually produce a severing of her bonds with the West and a movement towards the Eastern camp. The quasi-neutralist stance bequeathed by de Gaulle continued into the 1970s, but virtually disappeared by the 1980s[15].

The foreign policy of the German Federal Republic has made a complete contrast to that of France. Having regard to the perilousness of her position facing the Soviet bloc, she placed ultimate reliance for her security on the Americans, and took pride in being considered to be the latter's staunchest ally on the Continent. The West Germans could not conceive of Europe on its own having either the strength or the will to be an effective alternative in the manner the French appeared prepared to conceive of it. The situation was made more difficult for the West Germans by their position in regard to East Germany and the 'lost lands' beyond[16]. It has been seen that, in spite of its apparent hardness, the eastern frontier was, in fact, being maintained by the bayonets of the two superpowers, and the situation was made potentially more dangerous by the fact that the post-war changes brought about by the power of the Soviet Union in Eastern Europe were still not recognized by the Federal Republic a quarter of a century after the end of World War II. Then in 1970 came a massive *volte face* in West German foreign policy. Chancellor Willy Brandt saw the advantages for his country of ending the confrontational situation in central Europe and stabilizing the region by a recognition of geopolitical reality. The Chancellor's *ostpolitik* was aimed at the normalization of relations between the German Federal Republic on the one hand and her eastern neighbours, in particular the German Democratic Republic, Poland and the Soviet Union, on the other. In the treaties which were subsequently signed between the three countries, the Federal Republic made a public act of contrition for the war crimes of the Nazis, recognized the frontiers which had been imposed in the east after World War II and, perhaps most important of all, recognized the existence of the GDR – until then contemptuously referred to as the 'zone' – within the conceptual framework of 'two German states, one German nation'. This made way for a new four-power treaty regularizing the situation of Berlin[17].

Bilateral negotiations and relationships of the sort here outlined with France and West Germany were far more acceptable to the Soviets than dealings with an integrated group of countries as a whole. The emergence of a European entity with the makings of a unitary structure were not at all to their liking, the more so since the grouping in many ways possessed the economic weight of a superpower (*see* Chapter 7). From the beginning the Soviets had refused to recognize the international legal standing of the Community, and would not sanction direct EC–Comecon trade negotiations. There was certainly a fear of collective Community muscle and also of the wider implications of European unity. This was related to fear for their own neo-imperial structure in Eastern Europe in view of the indubitable attractiveness to the countries of the region of developing closer relationships with the Community. The Community's common external trade policy, which came into force in 1968, made possible the negotiation of bilateral agreements with Third World countries over a wide range of economic matters. Romania, the international maverick of the Eastern bloc, took advantage of this and negotiated such a trade agreement with the Community in 1966. As has been observed, the GDR has free access for its exports to the Federal Republic as a consequence of the latter's insistence that the countries are but two parts of one German nation. The Soviet Union itself is in many ways in a weak position economically. It has need of foodstuffs, manufactured goods and, above all, advanced techniques and technology from the West, much of this emanating from the Community itself. On the whole, the Eastern bloc needs the Community economically more than the reverse. This is the opposite situation from that which exists between the Community and the OPEC countries. Nowhere is the Community's autonomous strength as a 'civilian power' more in evidence than here, since in military terms its relationship with the Eastern bloc is bound up with that of the defence of the West as a whole.

As the Community has been evolving internally into an increasingly cohesive unit, it has also been developing new relationships with the rest of the world. These are different aspects of the same process, arising from the changed position of Europe since World War II. In 1950 what is now the Community consisted of ten sovereign states, each one having quite a different set of relationships with the other countries of the world. Most of them still looked outside maritime Europe in order to satisfy their national aspirations and to correct their inherent weaknesses. The great change which has taken place since then is their reorientation towards Europe; their policies have increasingly become regional rather than global. Around this, forming a sort of cocoon, there has been their relationship with the other countries of the Western world. The close integration within the Community is in many ways merely one aspect of the development of this wider relationship, and it has arisen from the operation of similar factors. It is geographical proximity and contiguity which have made them so much more intense within the Community.

At the same time as the economic, political, military and cultural ties within the West have been increasing, those between Europe and the 'South', mainly represented by the territories of the old empires, have been tending to diminish. This has arisen both from the disintegration of the maritime empires and from a fundamental change in world trading patterns. The growing gulf between Community North and ex-colonial South has been bridged since the 1960s by the Yaoundé and Lomé Conventions together with Community aid to the remaining dependent territories. The Community's main concern has been demonstrably with Africa, and especially with the countries of Black Africa. This stems from the fact that the colonial empires of the EC(6) were mainly in Africa, and the French in particular successfully persuaded the others to concentrate their developmental action on them. The high degree of concentration into a contiguous geographical area has certainly facilitated a more transnational and integrated approach by the Community's development agencies.

Such a degree of regional concentration is not considered by all as being the best way in which to conduct the relationship between the developed and the less developed world. The United Nations Conference on Trade and Development (UNCTAD) and the Brandt Report[18] both stress the desirability of a wider and more radical approach to the whole question of development. Yet the Yaoundé/Lomé approach certainly accords with the underlying premise of the Community itself, which is that regional cooperation among a limited group of adjacent countries is more realistic and likely to be more effective than are idealistic attempts at global action. Most of the ACP countries are very poor and have some of the most intractable development problems to be found anywhere[19]. This 'Fourth World' has been by no means an easy place in which to concentrate the Community's development policy.

The 'three crescent' structure of Community external relationships was given a severe jolt by the precipitation by the Arabs of the oil crisis in 1973. This small section of the primary-producing South, possessing supplies of one commodity vital to the developed countries, revolted against its subordinate status in relation to the West, and successfully and radically altered the balance of economic power in its favour. This has been seen by many as a forewarning of a more thorough-going change in the relationship between West and South. The thrust of the policies advocated and promoted by UNCTAD, OPEC, Lomé and the Brandt Report is to bring about just this kind of redistribution between the global rich and the global poor. Ultimately this process must lead towards a more equitable division of the world's wealth and profoundly affect the development of the relationship between the Community and Africa.

The European Community, together with its *de facto* associates in EFTA, is encapsulated within the American-led Western world, but has its own special relationship with the adjacent section of the Third World. Its relationship with the United States, within the general framework of the Atlantic Alliance, is largely one of client, while the Lomé group in turn is largely in an unwilling client relationship with the Community. The evolution of these two important relationships is a key to the Community's world role in the future. The central question is whether the Community will remain as a limited functional grouping, a 'civilian power' at most within the American orbit or whether it will move in the direction of autonomy, becoming a global superpower with its own *stratégie tous azimuts*. What proved unattainable for France in the 1960s could prove quite possible for a unit of five times its size. It has the potential strength, but whether it has the potential cohesiveness and political will is a very different matter.

Notes

1. 'The glory of foreign policy was identified with Empire and Commonwealth; its problems and perils with the continent of Europe. It was Czechoslovakia – in the heart of Europe – which Chamberlain described as a small, faraway country of which Britons knew little, after a century and a half of fighting on the borders of India'. Henry Kissinger in an address to the Royal Institute of International Affairs, London, on 11 May 1982
2. *See* Chapter 1, note 13

3. As a part of the Greater Reich (*Grossdeutsches Reich*) following the *anschluss* of 1938, Austria was treated as an ex-enemy country and in 1945 was divided, like Germany, into four zones of occupation. The Austrian State Treaty of 1955 gave Austria its independence, but stipulated that it had to remain permanently a neutral state

4. Following the signing of the Treaty of Accession in January 1972, Norway held a referendum. The result of the voting was that 53.5 per cent (1 099 389) of the total poll was against membership, and 46.5 per cent (956 043) in favour. Norway therefore did not ratify the Treaty of Accession

5. The participants in these summits are the German Federal Republic, France, the United Kingdom, Italy, the United States, Canada and Japan

6. '. . . the solution, in my view, is not to sacrifice the special intimacy of the Anglo–American connection on the altar of the European idea, but rather to replicate it on a wider plane of America's relations with all its European allies, whether bilaterally or with a politically cohesive European Community' (Henry Kissinger, op. cit.)

7. The eighteen signatories to the Yaoundé Convention were Benin, Burundi, Cameroon, Central African Republic, Chad, Congo-Brazzaville, Gabon, Ivory Coast, Madagascar, Mali, Mauritania, Niger, Rwanda, Senegal, Somalia, Togo, Upper Volta and Zaire

8. The idea of 'Eurafrica' was discussed in the foregoing chapter as part of a possible new 'frontier' of development. The political attitudes in Africa in the wake of independence rule this out entirely, at least in a structural way

9. The Suez Canal was vital at the time to the provisioning of Western Europe. Supplies fell sharply after the blocking of the canal, and it was a long time before the situation could be restored. It also demonstrated that shows of force in the old imperial style were not only inappropriate but probably doomed to failure in the post-imperial world

10. Known also as the Yom Kippur War, after the Jewish Day of Atonement on which it began. Having failed to dislodge the Israelis from the occupied territories, the Arabs then decided to invoke their massive economic strength, the 'oil weapon', against the West

11. *See* Chapter 5, note 2

12 Russia has been invaded four times from the west since the beginning of the eighteenth century. This has come to be regarded by the Russians as their 'invasion routeway', similar to France's eastern *pont des invasions*. The two most recent invasions were by the Germans, and fear of Germany has certainly been a very real one in the Soviet Union

13. France left the Council in July 1965 and did not return until January 1966. She agreed to do so under the terms of the 'Luxembourg Compromise', which diminished the supranational character of the Communities and maintained the veto on new initiatives and policy changes

14. Literally 'strategy in all directions', a policy of seeking independence from either bloc. It was finally abandoned in the early 1970s when it was seen that France's interests were inextricably bound up with those of the West in general. In spite of this, France has not returned to the command structure of NATO

15. This was one aspect of French foreign policy which was at the time firmly dedicated to the proposition that the nation was ultimately sovereign and completely free to take decisions

16. After the defeat of 1945 and the adjustment of the frontiers, it is estimated that some 11.7 million Germans were expelled from the lands to the east of the Oder–Neisse Line. Over 8 million of these eventually got to West Germany, and remained an active and vocal pressure group for the return of these lost lands to Germany. See R. E. H. Mellor, *The Two Germanies*, London, 1978

17. *See* Chapter 2, note 13

18. *North–South – A Programme for Survival:* Report of the Independent Commission for International Development Issues. Chairman: Willy Brandt, London, 1980

19. The GDPs of these countries are very low. Examples are

	$ million
Kenya	3280
Zambia	2200
Zaire	3510
Madagascar	1870
Chad	510

The figures are for 1976

Chapter 9

State, nation and region: the internal geopolitical structure

In discussing their relationship with the rest of the world the European Communities have been implicitly considered as a unit. Yet after all the time that has elapsed since the first treaty was signed in 1951, they still consist of a group of states which retain their ultimate sovereignty and their right to freedom of action. They have voluntarily surrendered control over certain aspects of their mutual economic relationships, but in other ways they act together by consent and ultimately by unanimity[1]. Voluntary interstate regional cooperation of this sort is so new a phenomenon that it is difficult to categorize it in the familiar political terms. It has been described as a loose form of international confederation, but it lacks many recognized confederal characteristics[2]. The central government of Canada, which is a modern example of a confederation, has far more power, especially in the field of foreign affairs, than do the institutions of the Community. The Holy Roman Empire has also been cited as a progenitor, and certainly the concept of the 'sovereignty' of the states within the overall 'majesty' of the empire comes closer to contemporary European realities. The fundamental purpose of any confederal grouping is to guard the independence of its constituent units, while at the same time facilitating the coordination of their mutual relationships. Such an association, forming a coordinated network of agreements, can act as agent for the maintenance of order within any contiguous group of states. The alternatives to such a positive relationship are either the slide into various permutations of international anarchy, the consequences of which were clearly demonstrated during the first half of the present century, or, alternatively, the imposition of unitary control from outside. It is significant that the Holy Roman Empire was ultimately destroyed by the growth and imperial expansion of two of its member states – Austria and Prussia.

It was the fear felt by her neighbours of just such a dominant position being achieved by Germany during the first half of the present century which was the backcloth to the establishment of the first Community. The new Franco–German understanding which dates from 1963 and which replaced three-quarters of a century of conflict was the centre of gravity of the new grouping. The surrounding states were attracted by this new pole of international stability, centring on what had been until then the continent's historic battleground. Since then the two countries have remained the key powers in the Community, and what they agreed at the beginning on iron and steel, coal production, agriculture, aid and links with the former colonies has underlain the direction of subsequent Community policy in these fields. That quadrilateral consisting of France, West Germany and Benelux is the Community's geographical, political and economic heartland, and within it are located the principal decision-making centres. It underpinned the Gaullist dream of reactivating the empire of Charlemagne with France as its motor, and with the massive, but now acquiescent, industrial strength of West Germany as its power base. However, France was in no position to secure a long-term pre-eminence of this sort, and the initiative tended in the 1970s to move eastwards across the Rhine to the country which has not only the greatest economic strength but is the Western alliance's front line against the Soviet bloc.

Since Italy has always been the weakest of the great powers, and remains so despite spectacular advances since the 1950s, the only effective counter-weight to the pre-eminence of France and Germany has been the United Kingdom. It has been observed that until well into the 1950s Britain was the strongest country, politically and economically, in Europe west of the Iron Curtain. As one of the victorious 'Big Three' and possessing still a world-wide empire she had the aura of a superpower on an altogether grander scale than the other European countries. From the middle of the 1950s there began that dramatic fall from this position, which continued into the 1980s. Her national income is now well below those of both France and West Germany; her per capita GDP is one of the lowest in the Community; her traditional industries are in chronic decline and, shorn of her imperial power base, she has reverted to the off-shore island of the nightmares of early twentieth-century statesmen. Her influence is further diminished by the fact that the British people have remained deeply divided on the question of Community membership, and the country has been widely regarded in Europe as being a half-hearted and unreliable partner. British disaffection has been made worse by the fact that she has been forced to accept a package of economic policies which were originally devised by the EC(6) and especially by France and West Germany, for their own benefit. An important effect of British membership has been to slow down the pace of integration, and British attitudes are shared by Denmark and Greece, both of which are also suspicious of the policies emanating from the centre.

The establishment of a rough balance of power between the largely integrationist centre and the more reluctant periphery has slowed down progress, and has in many ways contributed to moving the Community in a more international than supranational direction[3]. The states themselves remain the principal international actors and, in the last analysis, they are able to mould the direction of progress or even halt it altogether. However, while they are the stones of which the edifice is being constructed, they are by no means themselves monoliths, displaying as they do deep internal divisions. As was established in Chapter 2, the willingness of states to become members of the Community tended to be in inverse proportion to their possession of firm state-type spatial characteristics. These are least in evidence in West Germany and the Benelux countries, and are most in evidence in the peripheral countries of Ireland, Denmark and Greece. Looked at transnationally, firm state characteristics appear least in those states and parts of states which are within the geographical area of the Rhinelands.

An important element which diminishes the homogeneity of the state is the existence of sub-state nationalism. An early twentieth-century example of this was the powerful set of nationalisms which caused the disintegration of the Austro–Hungarian Empire in 1918. Within the European Community itself the power of Irish nationalism effectively broke up the United Kingdom, and was responsible for the birth of the Republic of Ireland in 1922. Today the most powerful sub-state nationalism is to be found in the 'Celtic fringe' of Scotland, Wales and Brittany. By the 1980s this had brought about a limited devolution of the internal power structures of the United Kingdom and, to a lesser extent, that of France. Belgium is, of course, completely divided between the Dutch-speaking Flemings and the French-speaking Walloons, each with their separate histories, cultures and mutual antagonisms. In addition to sub-state nationalisms of this sort, there are also the strong historically based regional feelings in Northern Ireland (Ulster), Alsace-Lorraine, Southern France, Bavaria, Corsica, Sardinia, Sicily and parts of Italy's Mezzogiorno. They are all powerful counterweights to sole identification with the 'nation state' itself.

Alongside, and often related to, the sub-state nations and regions there are the internal governmental structures. The powers vested in the sub-state vary considerably throughout the member states of the Community. Increased power and centralization of the state apparatus has gone hand in hand with the development of other state spatial characteristics, and evidence of this is to be found in varying degrees in every member country. Such centralization of power is also connected to the development of aggressive behaviour by the state. German aggression in the first half of the century was paralleled by a great increase in the power of the German imperial state at the expense of the rights of the historic units out of which it had been created in 1871. It was in response to the fears inherent in this interpretation of events that the new state created in 1949 out of the three Western zones was a federal one. In it the constituent *Länder* were given considerable powers over education, policing, industry and planning, and the authority of the West German government was strictly limited. This devolved political structure has since encouraged a rebirth of those provincial loyalties which had been so repressed under the Third Reich.

Similarly, the Italian constitution of 1948 divided the country into 20 *regioni*. At the time only five of them were actually given full constitutional powers, these being Valle d'Aosta, Trentino–Alto-Adige, Friuli–Venezia Giulia, Sicily and Sardinia. In 1970 the constitutional provisions for regional autonomy were implemented throughout the rest of the country and fifteen new *regioni* were established. They have elected councils with substantial powers in regional affairs, but many of them suffer the disadvantage of being far too small to act as real counterweights to central government. The United Kingdom is basically a unitary, not a federal, state, the only major exception to this being that under the Irish settlement of 1923 the 'six counties' of Ulster, which elected to remain a part of the United Kingdom, were granted a high measure of autonomy with their own governor and elected parliament. Direct rule was imposed in 1972 as a result of the troubled state of the province, but a return to devolved government, within the context of the 'Irish dimension' remains the British government's policy. As a response to the growth of political nationalism in Wales and Scotland, particularly following World War II, limited powers have been devolved to government agencies in Cardiff and Edinburgh. The government's proposal to implement a more thorough-going federalism was rejected by both electorates in 1979. The Maude Report of ten years earlier had proposed the setting up of an intermediate tier of regional council's between central and local government, after the models of the *Länder* and *regioni*. However, this was rejected largely because 'regional' loyalties, in England itself at least, have proved to be very limited. In Belgium, the strength of feeling in the two linguistic groups has forced the government there to make concessions. The cultural councils established in 1971 gave the *de facto* reality a *de jure* permanence, and it was the intention to channel the aspirations of the two communities into cultural rather than political fields.

Thus, in tandem with the rise and development of the Community ideal of close cooperation at the international level, there has been within a number of the member states an internal redistribution of power in favour of the provinces. If this process were to continue it could result in the effective break-up of some states and in the re-emergence of some historic provinces onto the international scene. There are many who welcome this development, and who see regionalism and internationalism as being, so to speak, reverse sides of the same coin. The thinking of the protagonists of this development is that the present states, and in particular the former great powers, are in fact not nations at all, but empires which were created by the conquest and absorption of the pre-existing nations. They postulate that the old sub-national units such as Wales, Bavaria, Burgundy or Alsace still have a powerful reality, often nearer to the people than are the imposed imperial states of which they have been forced to become a part. It can be maintained that such units are on a more human scale, that they still evoke real historical and cultural loyalties and that they are better equipped to deal with local interests than are governments in remote capitals often located hundreds of miles away. The link between this and the Community as a whole is the contention that such small units are likely to be more satisfactory partners than the larger powers have generally proved to be. The imperial states do, in fact, have a very poor track record in this respect, as the continent's recent history of bloodletting indicates. Proudhon considered the most acceptable units from the international standpoint to be 'groupes médiocres'[4]; they are unlikely to be powerful enough to pursue their interests independently and aggressively after the manner of the great powers, and so need the support of the international community. As Kohr has put it, 'Only the small states are wise, sensible and, above all, weak enough to accept an authority stronger than theirs'[5]. There is much evidence from the global international bodies, the League of Nations and the United Nations, to support the contention that small states, on the whole, tend to be better internationalists than are the large ones. The latter are still notoriously prone to the disease of *folies de grandeur*, and then to use their muscle in a bullying fashion to achieve their ends. If it is true that small states make better international partners than do large ones, then it is also likely to be true that they may also press forward more vigorously on the European front[6].

This, then, is one model for a Europe engaged in the process of unification – a Europe made up of regional states of modest size and having a vested interest in the maintenance of strong but democratic supranational institutions. This would not be a reactivation of the empire of Charlemagne, still less that of Napoleon, but of a kind of secular Holy Roman Empire possessing firmer institutions and without its expansionist Prussias or Austrias. Is it realistic at present to contemplate the possibility of an evolutionary development of so radical a kind in the Community? There has been considerable revival of interest in the sub-state units, in no small part due to the failures of the established states themselves and the perception of their responsibility for the holocaust of the 1940s. In spite of this, popular support for radical measures of devolution has been limited and erratic. The Irish experience of prolonged subversive activity followed by the attaining of independence from the imperial power derived from extreme conditions which do not have much of an echo in contemporary Western Europe. The present attitude to nationalism in Wales and Scotland demonstrates this difference clearly, and active support for Breton, Provençal or Bavarian nationalism has in recent times been confined to relatively small, though vociferous, minorities. Another factor is the high level of integration within the established states, facilitated by improved communication and by the draining of the peripheries in favour of the central regions[7]. The phenomenon of *Paris et le désert français* is an extreme example of a more widespread phenomenon deriving from the power of the modern state and the inequalities inherent in its territorial organization. This tendency to *désertification* of the peripheries and their domination by the centre has often made them too weak economically, politically, demographically and even culturally to be able to mount effective support for more than the most limited redistribution of power. When this occurs they will have been effectively integrated into the centre-dominated state system, and have largely acquiesced in their subsidiary role within it[8].

However, sub-state nationalism and regionalism could again capture the popular imagination more widely, so impelling central governments to launch further internal redistributive changes within their territories. Such a development could lead to the dismemberment of two Community states, the United Kingdom and Belgium, together with peripheral but significant adjustments to the structures of France and Italy. One could, in these circumstances, conceive of the creation of another five or even nine small states within the territory of the Community[9]. This would still leave eight of the existing member states largely intact, and England, possessing half of the territory and over three-quarters of the population of the United Kingdom, would remain a strong and powerful state. In two of the larger states, West Germany and Italy, considerable power is already devolved to the regions. Both are now far too homogeneous for movements to split them up further to have very much chance. The existing small states of the Republic of Ireland, Denmark, the Netherlands, Luxembourg and Greece would undoubtedly be acceptable members of a federal European state along lines such as those advocated by Kohr.

This still leaves France, the largest and most highly centralized state in the EC(10). It was the state around which the Community formed, but since the 1950s it has set greater store on national sovereignty. De Gaulle's *Europe des patries* concealed the vision of a Francocentric Europe, compensating the French for their loss of overseas empire. Since de Gaulle this has given place to a Europe in which all states would be equal, but the

Figure 9.1 France and its nations. Reproduced from *The Economist*, 16 September, 1978 by kind permission of the Editor and Publishers

heirs to de Gaulle may still have the glimmer of a hope that France could be more equal than others. A confederation of small to medium states in which France would be the strongest unitary power would thus be a very congenial situation to her. It would also be very much in accord with the French policy, pursued intermittently since World War I, of replacing big, bad and powerful Germany with good, little and weak Germanies. This is a possible future scenario on the basis of an acceleration of trends in the direction of undermining the cohesiveness of the present state structures. However, if one carries on still further down this road, one finds that even centralized France has its old pre-revolutionary provinces which are not that far beneath its neatly departmentalized surface (*Figure 9.1*). As Fouéré has put it, 'It was the sword which put an end to the independence of Burgundy, Brittany, Toulouse, and Dauphiné'[10] and, in spite of being 'devoured' for centuries by Paris, they could still have the energy to re-emerge if regionalism were again to become attractive in Europe. Certainly the anonymous and even hostile modernity of the contemporary national core regions is beginning to make the 'provinces' – whether they be the Dordogne, the Black Forest or Wessex – more attractive as places of habitation. As yet, whatever the protagonists may say, there appears little sign of this happening except in a toned-down intra-state manner, but the movement of political ideas is notoriously difficult to predict.

In addition to the effects of the sub-state political units there is also that of the great transnational centre, the Rhineland. As has been seen, this is central, economically strong and cosmopolitan, besides being the home of the Community's principal decision-making centres. Identification with the structures of the 'imperial' states is here also for the most part at a low level. As with the sub-state movements, the flowering of this transnational region since World War II is founded on the pre-state situation. It remains the geopolitical focus, and in many ways model, of transnationalism, and the centre of those counteractive forces to the power which is still strongly vested in the states themselves.

The political evolution of the Community between the 1950s and the 1980s has been away from the germ of true supranationalism and towards a more classic international balance of the interests of the member states. Linkages and trade-offs have often replaced the will to create new transnational structures. In many ways the old European balance of power has been reappearing in a new form within the framework of the Community. The stronger and more dominating states have since the 1960s become less inclined to surrender their control over events, and have attempted rather to steer the Community in the direction most in accord with their own national interests. Thus we have had France with her dreams of hegemony after the manner of Charlemagne or Louis XIV, West Germany getting Community support for the pursuit of her *ostpolitik* and Britain, her imperial power-base now pulled from under her, seeing the Community as a possible accession of strength while still preserving her wider global options. Neither France, Britain, nor even West Germany, has been able to forget that they have in the past been among the world's greatest powers, and in many ways they attempt to relive – perhaps almost unconsciously – their former roles through the Community.

In place of this balancing of national interests it is possible to envisage an internal political restructuring as a means of achieving a *relance* of true Europeanism. As Fouéré put it, 'Before becoming a European . . . you must first be born a Breton, a Fleming or a Provençal'[11]. Europe for the small nations and states is not so much extra muscle for the pursuit of national interests as a fundamental condition for their existence, a protective cocoon in which they can more easily flourish. The way in which Ireland, the Netherlands, Belgium and Luxembourg have seen European unity as being a liberating force and a surer safeguard of their national independence gives some indication of the attitudes of small states. Fouéré presents the 'small states' argument forcefully when he says,

> The Third Europe can be born only if we are prepared to accept the view that the great centralized states are a regrettable accident of European history, abnormal and transitory constructions which have outlived their usefulness and must be dismantled before resuming the march forward . . . They must cast their old skins and completely transform their internal structures: first of all, they must be broken up.[12]

The persistence of the worship of the sovereign power of the state is far more in evidence in Paris than in Athens, in London than in Dublin. It is in the heartland of the Community and around its peripheries that, for quite different reasons, identification with and loyalty to the states as now established is at its weakest. In the centre there is the overwhelming sense of something wider and bigger, while in the peripheries it is rather a sense of something smaller and nearer. It is in the great girdle between the centre and the peripheries that lie the heartlands of Fouéré's 'imperial states', the

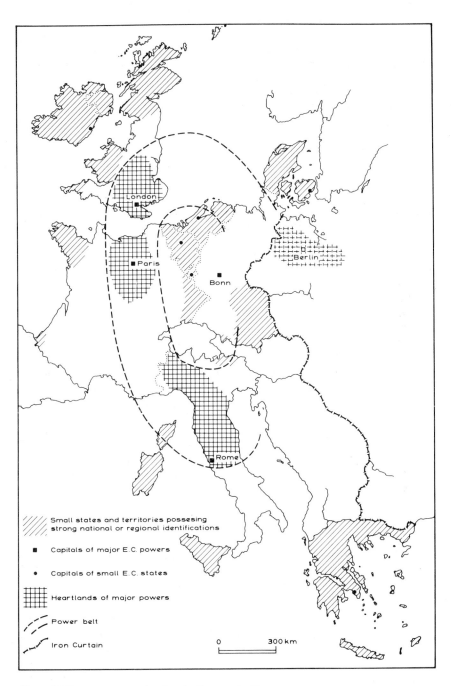

Small states and territories possesing
strong national or regional identifications

■ Capitals of major E.C. powers

• Capitals of small E.C. states

Heartlands of major powers

Power belt

Iron Curtain

0   300 km

London

■ Paris

Bonn

Berlin

Rome

Figure 9.2 Powers, states and nations in Community Europe

remains of that 'concert' of powers which dominated Europe and much of the world for so many centuries (*Figure 9.2*). Heritages of this sort inevitably die hard, and the echoes of Waterloo and Austerlitz, of imperial conquest and national glory resound in chancelleries which have now for long been concerned with more humdrum matters[13]. The battle between the ghost of imperial nationalism and the new continental supranationalism, between the evocative deeds of the past and the seemingly duller realities of the present, is most in evidence in the national heartlands of this girdle. It is especially to be seen in those of England and France, the last survivors of the Eurocentric global tradition.

The centre and the peripheries – Europeanism and provincialism – can thus be regarded as being two sides of the same coin. They now appear as unwitting allies in the creation of the new Europe against the girdle of great power heartlands which, so long after their real pre-eminence has passed, still retain considerable power, and popular support for a jingoistic nationalism which at times appears still to be only just beneath the surface.

Notes

1. This was the most salient feature of the 'Luxembourg Compromise' reached by the EC(6) in January 1966. *See also* Chapter 8, note 13
2. 'Federalism is not a clear-cut doctrine . . . it is in fact the art of dealing with realities in the best possible way.' *See* D. de Rougement, *The Idea of Europe*, London, 1966. The word 'pre-confederation' has been used to denote a coming together of sovereign states
3. An example of this was the effective institutionalization of the periodic summit conferences of heads of government. These became the European Council in 1975 and became a part of the institutional apparatus of the Communities
4. P. J. Proudhon, *Du Principe Fédératif*, Chapter VIII, Paris, 1863
5. L. Kohr, *The Breakdown of Nations*, London, 1957
6. This is not entirely borne out in the EC. The three Benelux countries have been consistently very much in favour of further European advance. Italy and Germany behaved like little countries in the 1950s because they were weak and defeated. Only France behaved like a great power in EC(6) and constantly attempted to have everything her own way. Finally, when this proved impossible, she halted the move to supranationalism by bringing about the 'Luxembourg Compromise' (*see* Chapter 8, note 13). As for EC(10), no distinct patterns emerge, although British attitudes to new initiatives during the first ten years of her membership were largely negative, and decidedly internationalist rather than supranationalist. While Ireland has thrown herself with a will into the Community, Denmark has been far less committed and enthusiastic about it
7. Myrdal contends that inequalities between regions have more to do with the process of cumulative causation than with the innate advantages or disadvantages of the regions themselves. Nothing succeeds like success and nothing fails like failure. *See* G. Myrdal, *Economic Theory and Underdeveloped Regions*, London, 1957
8. An example of this 'draining effect' is Wales. Its population of 2.8 millions gives it an overall density of population of 120 per km^2, compared with England's 350 per km^2. Since 1920 it is estimated that over one million Welsh people have migrated to England, this naturally leading to their effective Anglicization. Even so, there was in the early 1980s a considerably higher overall unemployment rate in Wales than in southern England. The 1981 census gave under 20 per cent of the population as Welsh-speaking, the majority being in the north and west of the principality; this compares with some 50 per cent in the early years of this century. In spite of this, in 1979 Wales rejected the British government's proposals for a limited measure of devolution, only 11.9 per cent of the poll being in favour

  9. Wales, Scotland, Northern Ireland, Flanders and Wallonia. Less strong, but potential candidates, would be Brittany, Alsace, Corsica and Sicily
 10. Y. Fouéré, *Towards a Federal Europe*, Swansea, 1980
 11. Ibid.
 12. Ibid.
 13. The Falklands War of 1982 is a good example of a temporary reversion to the former imperial role. The widespread national enthusiasm paralleled that for wars in the past, and was significantly greater than has been shown in Britain for the development of a peaceful apparatus to manage international relations

Chapter 10

Ideals and realities: the Community method and its future

The European Communities have been viewed in this book as constituting a continuous international process which began with the conceptual revolution of 1950. From this point on they became evolutionary, rather than revolutionary, a continuum leading in the direction of that ill-defined 'unity' for which European idealists had sought over the centuries. The method is functionalist, basing itself on the conviction that successful cooperation in one area will inevitably produce a spin-off into others, producing peace by pieces. Its history to date has not been one of steady uninterrupted evolution, but rather of a series of steps, periods of intense development followed by stagnation and even retrogression. World War II was the *dénouement* of unfettered statism, and the Community method was the new idea which gave hope for a break out of the destructive cycle of violence and conflict. The basic process occurred between 1950 and 1957, when the international situation, the 'soup', was just right. At the end of wars there has always come the cry that it must never be allowed to happen again. Now, adding weight to this, there were the external threats, from the American economy on the one hand and from the Russian tanks on the other.

The catalytic region in which the new international process was activated was the old Middle Kingdom, Lotharingia, which in the past had been the object of so much fighting. It had been the cockpit of Europe, but now it became the bridge from which the continent's new course was charted. 'Great crises are great federators,' said Monnet, and the extremity of the mid-twentieth-century crisis was the catalyst for the most effective international action since the nation state had become established. On witnessing the apparent success of the new pole of international cooperation, neighbouring states were attracted towards it, but there is little to suggest that these peripheral states would themselves have been inclined to internationalism had it not been for the initiatives emanating from this centre.

The rewards to Western Europe which have followed from the charting of this new course have been considerable. Peace and institutionalized cooperation replaced war and confrontation as the norms of West European international conduct. The Schuman Declaration had anticipated that in the new conditions war would become not merely unthinkable but materially impossible. The other promised reward for embarking upon this course of action was increased material prosperity for the peoples of Europe. This contention had been based upon the belief that a large economic unit would be inherently more effective than the smaller ones of which it was composed. In these the factors of production, land, labour and capital had become inefficiently deployed. In a continental-sized economic unit the factors would be able to move without restriction to those places where their efficiency could be maximized. The spatial dimension of this process was regional specialization in those areas within which the production of particular goods and services would be carried on most efficiently. The individual states, and particularly the larger ones, produced a very wide range of goods, and their industries were protected by tariff walls. This territorial insulation had been exacerbated by the increasingly autarchic policies pursued by governments during the first half of the twentieth century. Levels of intra-European trade had become far lower than one might expect from countries in such close physical proximity to one another. In 1938 the mutual trade of the EC(6) countries was only one-fifth of their total and by 1950 it was just over a quarter. It was contended by the protagonists of the Community idea that economic autarchy of this sort not only made the countries of Europe potentially more hostile to one another but also much poorer than they might otherwise have been. The two were clearly related, in that economically unsuccessful countries have in the past tended to be more belligerent. The release of the considerable economic potential could thus be expected to have wider international repercussions.

All this constituted a powerful argument for the extension of the economic aspects of the Community. The age of 'miracles' in the 1950s appeared proof of the relationship within the EC(6) between European unity and economic prosperity. This argument was made more convincing as a result of the relatively poorer performance of Britain. However, in spite of this, the economic arguments did not have that widespread acceptance accorded to the peace aspects. The 'anti-marketeers', most of them outside the EC(6) itself, disputed the assertion that a large integrated economic unit will automatically produce prosperity. Certainly, it is true that a facile correlation between prosperity and Community membership can no longer be sustained. There are now relatively poorer countries within the Community and there are richer ones outside it. The EC(10) faces considerable problems within its own territory, and it has been contended by 'anti-marketeers' that Community policies could actually tend to exacerbate these. Thus sectoral problems can be directly attributed in some instances to the free trade and competition within the Community, and enormous sums of money are consumed in subsidizing relatively inefficient agriculture. Even more fundamentally, the whole of the centre–periphery structure inevitably produces a rather dismal prospect for certain regions. It is clear that if the Mezzogiorno is peripheral in relation to the Italian peninsula itself, then the problems inherent in this geographical situation are likely to be magnified when viewed in the context of Europe as a whole. The statists thus contend that the state remains a better unit of organization than the continent, and that the states should, without prejudice to measures of regional cooperation, retain the right to determine their own policies in their own particular national interests. It is interesting that such nationalist approaches have tended to be more identified with the political parties of the left within EC(10). In this they frequently have allies on the extreme right, but it is the parties of the centre and centre-right which have traditionally been the Community's staunchest supporters.

In addition to the regionalist supporters of the Community and its statist (nationalist) detractors there are the globalists, who collectively constitute a third viewpoint on contemporary European affairs. They maintain that it is world-wide international arrangements, in the political, environmental and other fields which should be sought after through the strengthening of the United Nations and other international bodies. To them 'spaceship earth' is a unified physical and human ecosystem, and mankind's arrangements should reflect this unity rather than contribute to divisiveness. Limited regional arrangements, 'rich man's clubs', are particularly deprecated since they are alleged to consume energies which could more usefully be channelled into world-wide cooperation. It is also maintained that survival in these dangerous times for mankind demands concerted action of the most vigorous sort.

The statists and the globalists have a common front in that the world is now organized – or rather disorganized – into over 150 sovereign states, and the necessity of some common arrangements among them is clearly recognized even by the most ardent of the statists. The statists also find globalism more acceptable, since the restrictions placed upon sovereignty by a global cooperative body will naturally be far looser than those which would be likely in a tighter regional grouping such as the Community itself. They also allow the state a wide range of options in the pursuit of its own particular interests without its being inhibited by binding supranational arrangements.

Thus, while there has been widespread acceptance that peace and constructive dialogue have been enhanced by the Community method, there is far less general agreement that it has been an unmitigated economic blessing, or that the Community should now move forward towards complete political unity. The question can be resolved into a choice between the two practical alternatives of a global organization of sovereign states or a submergence of the states into new macroregional units. The wider alternatives of unfettered statism or total globalism are too unrealistic to merit serious consideration on their own.

Globalism in practice does not have an impressive track record. The fundamental failure of the League of Nations arose from its sheer size. States did not identify their interests closely with far-flung places on the other side of the globe. They were shown to be generally far more concerned with what was occurring in their own regional neighbourhoods. The great powers, which did have global interests and responsibilities, could not be controlled by the League, any more than they have been controlled since 1945 by the League's successor, the United Nations. In contrast to these failures, since World War II macroregionalism has become a significant force in world affairs. In the 1950s the Eurocentric empires had begun to give place to new states, and there developed a tendency for them to seek mutual cooperation within their regions. This has been a widespread phenomenon designed to correct their inherent weakness, vulnerability and economic inadequacy. Such groupings include the countries of Black Africa (OAS), the non-Communist countries of south-east Asia (ASEAN), the Arab countries (Arab League) and Latin America (ANDEAN and others). The degree of success has been limited, but the will to achieve greater strength and well-being through regional cooperation has been a potent driving force in their actions. Consciously or unconsciously, they appear to be striving towards emulating the large states themselves, just as one strand of European thinking envisages Europe as evolving into a kind of superpower.

Faure's world order dominated by 'les quatre grands' was extended by Richard Nixon, who in the 1960s talked of a 'pentagon' of powers which would include these four, together with Japan. It is suggested by others engaged in the study of global *realpolitik* that these five northern mega-powers could be dominating the world in the twenty-first century much as western Europe did in the nineteenth. However, it is possible to take this thinking a stage further; extending regional cooperation throughout the world could lead eventually to far more such new powers. The Arabs, the states of south-east Asia and those of Latin America clearly have potential in this direction. One would anticipate a ranking of such new regional powers as there was in nineteenth-century Europe. This regional coopera-tion is also likely to be promoted not simply as a direct consequence of geographical proximity but by the ethnic and cultural similarities which such proximity produces over a long period of time.

The creation of regional groupings cannot realistically be regarded as being an inevitable consequence of the presence of the geographical, historical, economic and other factors. Strong similarities had existed in Europe before 1950, but this had not prevented a steady drift apart, interspersed by periodic bloodlettings. The geofusive process in Western Europe was activated by circumstances caused by the coincidence of certain geographical and historical factors. They formed a unified geopoli-tical field consisting of a chain from war and its aftermath through the birth of the idea to the formation of the new state. These factoral links were all clearly present in Western Europe in the late 1940s and early 1950s. Idea met reality, and the catalyst produced a positive geofusive reaction. It set in train the continuing process of the subsuming of existing units into a single large one. The kinetic potential for geofusion had been converted into a dynamic process, and by the 1980s it had profoundly altered the entire international situation in the European maritime crescent. The process is taking place at many speeds, strongest in the centre and weakest in the peripheries. Even states on the edges of the crescent, such as Turkey and Finland, have been profoundly affected by developments at the centre. It is not part of the object of this book to examine the extent to which all the elements in the unified field are present in other processes of regional cooperation. It would seem that the elements of the field were present more intensely in Europe, the old heart of the occidocentric world, than elsewhere, and the geofusive process began earlier and was initially more successful. Furthermore it was built, as has been seen, on unique physical foundations.

The 'three crescents' of world involvements which were outlined in Chapter 8 indicate the Community's westerly and southerly orientation, the strongest manifestations of which are the Atlantic Alliance and the Lomé Conventions. These are twin 'special relationships', one with that part of the Third World with which the Community has been most recently and closely involved, and the other with the superpower of the geostrategic region of which it forms a part. Yet despite the clear maritime and westward external orientation, internally the spatial evolution of the Community has been tending to develop an easterly component. As was seen in Chapter 1, following the collapse of *Mitteleuropa* in 1945, the maritime and continental peripheries were drawn into the vacuum produced by the eclipse of the continent's central geopolitical region (*Figure 1.1*). The zone down the middle separating the two then became a sort of fortified desert, from which the civilian activities in adjacent countries tended to draw back. This is particularly evident in the westerly spatial orientation of the German Federal Republic. However, since the West European economic recovery of the 1950s, those countries nearest to the central section of the Iron Curtain have tended to become the most successful. It is the countries of that middle European zone stretching from Scandinavia through West Germany and on to the Alps which have been economically strongest and in some ways politically more stable. Besides the fact that they are all in the central zone, they are also for the most part modern, with a concentration on the production of high value-added consumer goods. They are protestant–secular in tradition, neutralist in sentiment and, significantly, Germanic in language and culture. To the south, east and west of this zone, general levels of economic well-being tend to decrease. It follows from this that the countries of the old maritime European geopolitical region have tended to become relatively less successful and powerful. The most dramatic manifestation of this is seen in the collapse of British power between the 1940s and the 1970s. Maritime areas adjacent to western *Mitteleuropa*, such as Benelux and eastern France, have been able to reorientate themselves in the context of new European developments, and the central axial belt in particular. As the reality of power has moved away from the maritime fringes, the British Isles and western France have tended to slip, as did the countries of the Iberian peninsula two centuries earlier.

This success of western *Mitteleuropa* adjacent to the Iron Curtain is mirrored by developments which have also taken place on the other side of the Iron Curtain. Here after World War II considerable redrawing of frontiers had taken place and, as the Soviet Union filled out her frontiers and established her *cordon sanitaire*, Poland, as Winston Churchill put it, was shunted like a railway carriage 200 km westwards. The most economically advanced countries of Comecon are those which, in the past, had come under the strongest influence from the Germanic powers of *Mitteleuropa*. The German Democratic Republic, Bohemia and western parts of Poland are the most industrialized and, since the 1960s, Hungary has also undergone a successful economic transformation. It is thus around the eastern fringes of the Iron Curtain, adjacent to the Community, that the most prosperous and advanced conditions are generally to be found. It has been seen that intra-German contacts have played an important part in this and have made the central parts of Europe's great divide a much softer frontier than might have been supposed from the confrontation of the superpowers.

Thus with the easterly orientation in the West and the westerly orientation in the East, there has been a distinct coming together in the spatial sense. The military drawing in of the 1940s has been followed imperceptibly by an economic drawing in since the 1960s. The overall western orientation of the Community exists together with this eastern backwash, and this has considerably altered the realities within the post-war central European desert. An extrapolation from existing trends would suggest that a new central Europe, a sort of economic *Mitteleuropa*, is in process of emerging (*Figure 10.1*). Such a development certainly accords with the formation of new units resulting from geofusion along previously hostile frontiers, such as occurred in the Rhinelands in the 1950s. Whether the geofusive factors will be activated in this area is likely to depend on the wider global situation, and in particular on the state of relations between the two superpowers. As has been stated, the physical presence of

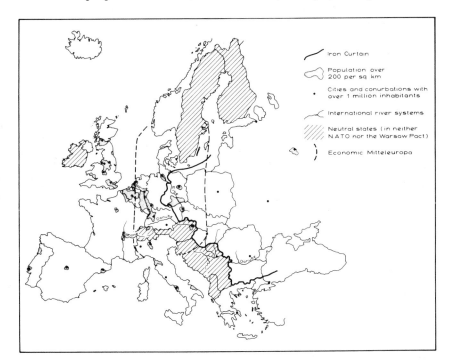

Figure 10.1 Present realities and future possibilities

favourable factors is not enough; what is needed is the catalyst which will activate them positively. Such a catalyst consists fundamentally of an union of the chronological with the chorological – the urgency of resolving a spatial problem within a particular time scale. Unless some entirely new factors were to enter the scene, the sort of spatial imbalances found in the EC(6) in the 1950s do not appear to be major intractable problems in the mutual relations of the E(26) at the present day. Of course, a coming together of Europeans in order to prevent their total destruction in a superpower confrontation could not be ruled out if the situation took on the required urgency. It would also depend on the superpowers refraining from intervening so as to prevent the geofusive process and to shore up 'glacis Europe' once more. Such a process, if it had a strong military purpose, could produce the reactivation on a large scale of *Festung Europa* or, if it took another course, it could lead to the emergence of a united civilian Europe.

Putting the movement towards European unity once more in the context of world developments, it has been contended that macroregionalism has emerged since World War II as a dynamic force, since countries throughout the world are embarked on a search for regionalist solutions to a variety of international problems. This is taking the form of clusterings of states around catalytic regions, and much trial and error is likely to be needed before they solidify into large regional states. In the cold light of reality, international macroregionalism of this sort appears as the true successor to the Eurocentric imperialism which dominated the world until well into the present century. Both statist nationalism and pan-globalism have also been significant forces since 1950 but, for quite different reasons, they have had little success in tackling the problems of the present-day world.

The developing macroregions present the prospect of peace and cooperation amongst neighbours, more readily enforced by regional authorities than by global ones, yet the economic viability of the 'big is beautiful' philosophy still remains open to question. In this controversial area, it must be remembered that the Community became economic because it was Monnet's narrow breach in the ramparts of sovereignty into which advance could most successfully be made. But it was always basically political, always about 'unity' in the widest sense. As Jean Monnet put it, he was not interested in coal and steel but in the unity of Europe. It could thus be that the economic preoccupations which were then forced on the Community, and which have since remained the very bread and butter of its existence, constitute in truth a *pis aller*. Many see the way forward as being a return to the mainstream of cooperation and movement towards a wider framework of unity. The macroregional (Community) authorities would concentrate on what they do best, while other matters, which could well include many which are at the moment the preserve of Community agencies, could possibly be more efficiently achieved by other means.

Much evidence suggests that what Fouéré has referred to as the imperial state is outdated, and should be encouraged to disappear. During recent times Hobbes' Leviathan has now in many ways degenerated into a dinosaur, which is impeding the movement towards those new political forms more appropriate to the present and the future. According to this thinking, the subversive agents would be Proudhon's *groupes médiocres*, which, it is contended, have a greater reality than the imperial states which in the past overcame them, and which now attempt to hold on to their diminishing power. This sort of Community would come to be based upon an alliance of the microregion and the macroregion, each of them having its own particular role. In this scenario de Gaulle's *Europe des états* would give place to Fouéré's *Europe des nations*, which would be the units of a new federal system.

All progress in international affairs is brought about by attempts to make adjustments in the interests of particular groups. The desire for such adjustments results from feelings of dissatisfaction with the existing order of things. These feelings may, in some cases, be confined to some limited or fanatical group which is in reality out of touch or sympathy with the great majority of the people. If, on the other hand, the desire for change has widespread popular support, then it may mobilize political energies to achieve the necessary adjustments. This may be accomplished peacefully, by kinetic means alone, but all too often such change has been sought by dynamic means, using force and so entailing war. On the international scene this will result if the adjustment is not acceptable to other states, possibly because the advantage accruing to the one may produce a disadvantage to another. Such an adjustment, if then brought about by force, is likely to sow the seeds of further conflict. It will produce the psychology of the vendetta in international relations. Strasbourg's wreath of *immortelles* represented the refusal to accept adjustments brought about entirely by *force majeur*. This vendetta psychology, this long memory for real or imagined wrongs, this desire for adjustment brought about inevitably at the expense of others, has been a central feature of international dynamics in Fouéré's 'second Europe' – the age of the state. The keynotes of the 'third Europe' which began tentatively in May 1950 are consent and agreement on changes, and the attempt to find common ground as a basis for moving forward without constant recourse to arms.

We are still in the age of overlap, when the force of nationalism, particularly in the erstwhile imperial powers, remains strong, while the forces of macroregionalist internationalism are still fledgling. After all, the third Europe is only just beginning. The Europe of states lasted over 300 years; France and England as political units are a thousand years old. Yet despite its youth, it is founded on geographical reality – on that reality of which both Monnet and Schuman were so conscious when they proposed beginning with limited functional cooperation. The chronological and the chorological dimensions of functionalism had their interface in this unified geopolitical field. From functional cooperation there was a move out into fresh fields in time and space in the search to establish peace by pieces.

Index